Will this house last forever?

Will this house last forever?

Xanthi Barker

TINDER
PRESS

All poems by Sebastian Barker are reproduced by kind permission of
Hilary Davies. Grateful acknowledgments are made to Enitharmon Editions,
publishers of *The Land of Gold* (2014) and *The Hand in the Well* (1996)
where these poems first appeared.

First published in Great Britain in 2021 by Tinder Press
An imprint of HEADLINE PUBLISHING GROUP

1

Cataloguing in Publication Data is available from the British Library

Hardback ISBN 978 1 4722 7444 1

Typeset in Scala by Palimpsest Book Production Limited,
Falkirk, Stirlingshire

Printed and bound in Great Britain by
Clays Ltd, Elcograf S.p.A.

Headline's policy is to use papers that are natural, renewable and recyclable
products and made from wood grown in well-managed forests and other
controlled sources. The logging and manufacturing processes are expected to
conform to the environmental regulations of the country of origin.

MIX
Paper from
responsible sources
FSC® C104740

HEADLINE PUBLISHING GROUP
An Hachette UK Company
Carmelite House
50 Victoria Embankment
London EC4Y 0DZ

www.tinderpress.co.uk
www.headline.co.uk
www.hachette.co.uk

For SSB

There's another world mixed in with this one.
  You see it when someone dies.
The holy spirit of life and death
  And the monumental lies.

'Double Take', Sebastian Barker

Contents

SSB's Dictionary

Presuppositionology: the study of what people presuppose. Particularly looking at the false or problematic assumptions underlying statements of fact or value judgements.

Paradoxical

31st January 2017

My dad is dead. He died three years ago. I miss him and I wish he hadn't died.

But he is also not dead, and the previous three sentences are all lies.

He is dead because he died on 31st January 2014. It's a recorded fact and you can find it on the internet – he was a poet, not famous, but known to some people, with his name on books you can buy. I have the receipt for his death certificate in a brown box made to look like an old-fashioned book on the shelf beside my bed.

But he is also not dead because I saw him this morning, waiting at a bus stop, and he gave me a wave.

And so though he is dead and I can't call him up, sometimes I am walking a long way and it is exactly what I do. His voice is the only right thing for that walk and he knows what I've called him for, and he's expecting me. He's still on my phone's list of favourite numbers so I can call him with one click, one press of the thumb, if I want to, but he is dead and nobody answers. But once in a letter addressed from the mountains of some-where I'd never been, in the blue ink of his heavy pen he wrote: 'I talk to you, but without a telephone line the words tend to go astray.' So like when I was a child and didn't hear from him for months, I don't believe that because he doesn't answer it means he isn't speaking to me.

It seems that he must be dead because he doesn't know anything about my life now. People with living dads have conversations in real time, discussions about work and Tube strikes and retirement plans. When someone says to me they are going to see their dad, a hollowness gapes invisibly in my chest and I can't say anything like, 'Oh yeah, dads, those old guys, all bad jokes and struggling with the internet.' I can only say disturbing things like, 'Just wait. When they die, the jokes get worse.' We never had a chance to talk about important things like becoming a parent or how to bleed a radiator or the way a mind smashes open like a gas canister or a supernova flaming out into the world when a person dies and you can't see them any more, how time opens up like a giant's mouth and swallows something you did not know you had, and you didn't know what it was, so haven't got the words to ask for it back, and that I got pregnant, and the mad shock of elections around the world and what he thinks of the EU or Donald Trump, in fact we never talked about politics at all. My dad is dead because he doesn't know anything about 2017, or 2016, or 2015 or most of 2014.

But he is also not dead because nothing has changed. I never would have talked to him about these things. He left when I was a baby and didn't visit all that much. When he did visit, he was easily bored and didn't like to talk about what he called personal matters. We would not have discussed work or my prickling anxiety, heaving overdraft, disappearing boyfriends, abortion. I would not have known about the giant's mouth, and I could not guess what edifying things he would have said about Trump. We talked about space–time and DNA and words he made up, like 'presuppositionology', and the first ever life forms on the planet – *chemolithoautotrophic hyper-thermophiles*, he says, *say it again, try again, slowly now, once more* – the majesty of aphids and the psychoactive quality of conversation, whether or not two people could ever be said to know each other. He is not dead, because we're still having these conversations, because I have the notes and letters he wrote as addenda, can open at any time all the footnoted emails he sent.

But he is also dead because now I talk to nobody about these things.

You might say that he is dead because he had a funeral. There was a church service and a burial and a wake and several guests. But it is also true that he didn't have a funeral because the funeral we attended was not his. People wore strange clothes and faces and did not say anything they meant. The hall was so large that nobody could fill it up, it was only an emptiness, and everybody felt conspicuous and sober. It was February, and cold, and there was nowhere to sit and the elderly guests complained. If my dad were to have a funeral, it would not be like this. He made the personal request to me years ago that Bruce Springsteen be played at his funeral, the song 'No Surrender'. In fact, I promised him. So he is not dead, because this has not happened yet.

When he dies, I know exactly what kind of funeral he would like and I will make sure to organise it right. He wants Pink Floyd and Bob Dylan and impassioned, drawled speeches made by scruffy, opened-up people drinking too much wine and stealing cigarettes and dancing. He's a poet and he'll have a poet's funeral. There were none of these things at the funeral I attended, except wine, but I learned from him years ago, before I knew what wine was, that it was a different thing drunk from glasses or a copper jug, and a different thing drunk with friends or people who didn't even know he had children. Also, though supposedly his face was on the funeral leaflet, it was a peculiar, irregular picture, like he was wearing someone else's expression, someone else's clothes. Several people commented he would have been dismayed. 'He was very vain,' his sister said, 'he would have wanted to look his best.' For this reason it is quite easy, even appropriate, to believe that it was not his, but a stranger's funeral.

On the other hand, he has a grave, and a gravestone with a line of his poetry carved into it. The stone is Welsh slate. It is smooth and earth-cold and hand-carved and when I visited the stonemason, there he was, going: *Look!*

Look at that – the way the mason's hand forms the letters straighter than a stencil, no need for a ruler, the way he sees through the tips of his fingers like an insect. He was dead because the stonemason could not see or hear him, because the stonemason knew nothing of him but the name he carved into the slate, because I had driven there with his wife, and we had not taken a trip alone together before, because it was six months since he had died, and I had been through the death-ache of it, and as my brother insisted: he was deader than dead – but he was also not dead because I heard him say it. He is not dead, because who I mean is *him* – the living one.

The living one: he's whispering at the back of my neck as I type this. I'm draped in the warm balm of his smile. He's my dad and I know him.

'Take the presence of your husband or your wife or your friend – of your loved ones', he wrote. 'Each is unique and obviously so.'

I can feel him here behind me. But he is also dead, because I can't touch him, and I am losing the memory of his shoulders, and the way he squeezed me against his side, and because I won't ever again walk into a room in which he is sitting and watch the space between us light up with the snap-magic that erupts when both our particular mouths go hello grinning.

He is dead because this is painful to think about.

But he is also not dead, because it is impossible not to think about. I can see every moment of him: rolling his sleeves up and reaching for his gnarly wooden hammer; his eyes half shut in his racing-green Rover singing Bob Dylan's 'Pat Garrett'; making toasted cheese sandwiches in a machine he used a clamp to keep shut; waving a glass of green wine in the late sunlight, a blanket tucked over his faded legs; smoking Rothmans and reciting his poetry, blind drunk, under the Greek sky two decades ago; eating a picnic at his desk on Father's Day, just before he got ill, while he explained his new poem to me and could not believe that I understood him, his joy making me lose any of the familiar resentment, and he said, 'What are you doing with your hair? Pulling your hair like that. That's just what my mother used to do.'

But he is dead because this is not the whole truth. There are things I don't want to remember: his silence, his absence, his indifference to our lives; hanging up on me when I said something he didn't like; telling me quite casually he hadn't wanted me, a fourth child. The mystic poet-wanderer and the cold, intellectual snob – how can I tell it isn't only the latter who died, and my real dad is hiding somewhere? The other died, and I'm not sad about it. I won't see him again and I don't mind one bit. I hated him, as I felt his hatred of me. But there is another dad, a realer dad, the dad I let myself remember, and I will wait for him forever as I've been waiting for him my whole life.

But he is also dead because I remember nothing.

I saw him lying on the floor. I felt the warmth go from his face. The paramedics cut off his T-shirt. Later other strangers put him in a bag and carried him to a van. It was hard to get him down the stairs and my brother went to help, trying to press his final love into strength and logistics, but it was traumatising, he said, he wished he hadn't gone. My dad would never have allowed this – not my brother's pain, he wouldn't have helped with that, but he would have found a better way to engineer the transportation. He could have solved things like that. Though he could not have solved the nauseating awkwardness of all of us, both intimate and unknown to each other – his daughters, his son, his wife and ex-wife – sitting there all day in that house which was no longer his, crying and shaking and not saying anything and then saying too much, talking about work and failed MOTs and the last time we'd each seen him and soup and nothing, my mother taking care of everybody, her own feelings stashed far outside the house. If he was not dead, there is no way my mother would have been in that house.

He is dead because he has always been dead. Death, abandonment, it makes no difference. He is dead because it is so typical of him, disappearing when I turn up to need him.

But he is also not dead, because it is hard to tell the difference, sometimes too hard, and I hate him for that and want him to die.

He is not dead because he would never give me what I wanted.

He is dead because I saw him in the chapel of rest. He was frozen. It was disturbing. His skin was like agar, like a dead jellyfish washed up on a manmade beach. But he is also not dead because he was there the day I first touched a dead jellyfish, first recorded this sense memory, and so he was there too, that day, looking over his own plasticised face with me, wondering what to say or do. He is not dead because it was him in me, looking at the him he was no longer in, thinking about the mechanisms of things, considering it necessary to know.

He is dead because they put him in a suit. He is dead because he didn't wear suits, not often. He wore trousers and tough cotton shirts tucked in but open so you could see his T-shirt. He wore T-shirts and jumpers, but mainly tough cotton shirts, and he was never cold. Never. Never that cold ever at all.

He is dead because they nailed the coffin and put him in a hearse, and because of that funeral, though it was not his funeral, and how heavy it was for the men to carry him in.

He is dead because they buried him, I was standing there, we threw in handfuls of soil and holy water from a plastic squeeze bottle with HOLY WATER handwritten on a sticky label on the side. But he is not dead because that bottle was absurd. He is not dead because none of it made sense. He is dead because death doesn't care about sense, and because we prayed and rode in limousines. But he is also not dead because out of the corner of my eye, standing there beside the swathe of lawn in the middle of the urban-sprawl grasslands in which they supposedly buried him, I saw him sail off into the silver-blue sky, heard him whisper-cry, *Let's go.* He is not dead because I don't believe it, and whoever tells me otherwise, I don't give a damn how they look back pitying, all-knowing, whatever they're thinking, I just remember that, see him up there, smile.

He is not dead because I saw him in the Hagia Sophia, one year later. He did an arabesque, gliding down the chandelier, after tiptoe-dancing around the multiplicity of religions, smoothing his way through Christ, Peter, Mary, the word of Allah, tourists, camera phones, gold leaf. He is not dead, because I doubled over right there and laughed until strangers were alarmed and my eyes watered and I had to sit down. He is not dead because it is just like him, these appearances, sudden and frank and winking and silent, and though there is so much more you want from him, you're not getting it, no matter what you do, and though you hate him for it you have to admit he does a spectacular job of making such a small thing gorgeous.

He is not dead because he has never been the kind for conventions, for obeying society's petty rules. *Dead?* he'll be saying. *Well sure – but have you thought about what that means?*

He is dead because I'm angry with him: this con-fusion is his fault, he was always filling up my head with fantastical thoughts, other worlds and possibilities he could never remain close enough to uphold, and because he abandoned my mother with two tiny babies and never said sorry and so he deserved it.

He is dead because he wanted to die, he was ready for it, grateful, when he heard.

He is dead because he drank himself to death.

He is dead because he'd had enough of life, and said so. He'd had enough of watching us grow up.

He is dead because he lived his life for metaphors. He is dead because he spent his life alone in a room, filling journals with meticulous handwriting and watercolours nobody ever saw. He is dead because he *is* a metaphor – what happens when you mistake writing for life.

But he is also not dead because this ambivalence is metaphysical, because it brings him back and keeps him changing and I no longer believe it is possible to die. But that being alive is just the finite tip of a person. And death is only a pit stop. A momentary collapse into nothingness before smashing back, straight through the sense of this ersatz fact: he died.

What happened first:
a love story

My mother first met you one Friday night in the spring of 1983 in a pub in Nottingham neither of you had been in before. You were staying with friends nearby because you were reading at a poetry festival the next day. My mother was a teacher there. But your friends happened to be her friends also, the only people she had met since moving to the city who could talk and laugh and think the way she needed to. You were sitting with your drinks at the table when she walked in, warmth already tumbling from between her blonde hair and denim jacket. When she sat down, you took off your glasses, looked straight at her. She didn't know then that you could not see without them.

She was twenty-six, had left home years before and had nothing to go back to. This job, this city was only a way to keep moving forward. She was desperate to get away from the feeling of frustration that clawed at her teeth. Usually she and her friends spent their weekends searching for whatever they could find – what life and conversation – drinking gin and listening to the Eurythmics, making each other laugh and swirling around the dance floor in the smoke. You were a decade older, a poet living from residency to residency, both shyer and bolder than my mother, as she was both shyer and bolder than you. You liked each other immediately.

That Friday night after the pubs closed, the four of you walked across the city in the rain back to your friends' flat. You talked to my mother and she talked to you. 'Total Eclipse of the Heart' had come out that week and you had both gone out immediately to buy it, could not get enough of listening to it. When you came back the next day, after your reading, you brought her a box of Turkish delight.

It wasn't long before you came back another weekend to see her. She cooked for you and you played each other records and the days disappeared and you could not stop talking, all these things my mother had never been able to say coming out of her mouth. And you could not believe how she made you laugh. And you could not believe how she made you think. And you could not believe how she made you feel, thirty-seven years old, but you had not felt that way before. How she looked at you. How she knew what you meant. You told her that the kind of poetry you were interested in had no home in England. You had to go to Greece, you said, where the poets had not lost their spiritual core. You wanted to buy an old house there, somewhere quiet, a village in the mountains far from anywhere, a ruin that you could rebuild, whatever you could afford. You were going there next month to look for somewhere, no you'd never built a house before. You had a glint in your eye, as though daring her to disbelieve you. As though all the unlikely things you said were not strange at all if looked at the right way. As though my mother was exactly the person to look at them like that. She told you how lost she'd felt, how hard it was to get where she wanted to be.

'You don't belong here,' you said. 'You're a fish out of water. Come with me. You could lend me a hand.'

It was months until the summer holidays but you wrote to her, as you said you would. You had found a place, a pile of stones that was once a house, centuries old, in a village way up in the mountains. You had bought it for the price of a used car and would start work on it immediately. You gave her the phone number for the village cafe and as soon as she'd reached the end of the last day of term, she changed a twenty-pound note into fifty-pence pieces and took them to the nearest phone box to ring you.

She waited, the large plastic receiver sticky at her ear, listening to it ring and ring. Her nerves crept in. What time was it in Greece? Her stomach churned in anticipation. There was someone waiting to use the phone. She was about to hang up, thinking to try again tomorrow, when a gruff voice answered.

'Ne? Ne?' followed by a tangle of Greek. The man sounded furious.

'Sebastian, Sebastian,' she repeated. Her third fifty pence dropped.

'Ne, ne,' the voice kept saying.

17

Was he saying no? But he sounded positive, not furious any more but welcoming. She did not know whether to hang up when the shouting was replaced by muffled voices and then a long silence. The phone clicked and she put in another fifty pence, and then another. Then the voices got louder and she heard someone clear their throat and then finally, you said her name.

Your voice, over the crackly line, was both changed and familiar. There wasn't much time left to speak. She told you she could come next week. 'Get to Kalamata,' you said. You'd pick her up there. That was the only instruction you gave her.

Like that, it happened.

Less than a week later my mother flew into Athens and found her way to the train station where she bought a ticket to Kalamata. In the fragments of language she could piece together, she understood the train would leave that night, arriving sometime in the morning. She waited on the darkening platform until the train arrived, a line of metal carriages clattering to a halt with no other passengers on board. Inside, she had to grip the edge of the spongy seats to keep from falling off them. The ill-fitting panes in the windows shook, the night air cutting through the gaps. This draught and her bewilderment kept her from sleeping and instead her tiring eyes tracked the landscape through the window as it got darker and darker.

In the early hours, the train ground to a halt and she

heard the conductor's muffled shouting. She was too tired to care why they were being held up. Her eyes were no longer focusing on the world outside when a dull thud sounded against the window opposite and she looked around to see two hands pressed against the glass and a face between them.

Your face. Your hands.

She sat up. 'Sebastian,' she said.

'Come on,' you said, 'get off the train.'

She dragged her bag out of the carriage and when her eyes found yours a huge smile spread over her face. 'Where are we?' she said.

The conductor appeared to slam the door behind her, waving at you in acknowledgment. Then the two of you embraced for the first time in months and the engine started up again, leaving the station deeper in the swallowing dark that surrounded it. You'd intercepted her train in a small town much closer to the village than Kalamata. The station was barely more than a stone arch, the Hillman Avenger you had driven over from England parked on the other side of it. You set off. The road had no street lights. My mother had never seen so many stars. As the road wound through the valley, the crickets hummed through the car's open windows and you told her what had happened so far.

You'd arrived at the pile of rocks, no words in Greek, no knowledge of stone work, roofing, how to tear down a mountainside of cacti. For the first week you didn't know what to do. You got up every day and walked down to the house and stared at the rubble. Rumours spread through the village. You were garnering cold stares and baffled tuts. One morning you set out early up the mountain, looking for fallen cypress trees to make new beams for the roof. You were ecstatic to find one, only a few miles up from the village, just the right size and length, and set about dragging it back. On entering the village you noticed crowds of people – it was Sunday, so you guessed they were churchgoers – but soon found yourself in the middle of a wedding. Imagine, you told her, a half-naked Englishman dragging a tree on his hip through the ceremony? You were scolded, but a couple of men helped you carry the trunk home, then ordered you back to join the party.

The next day when you went to stare at the rubble, you noticed children gathering to watch. The day after, they were back again. And the next day too, a little closer this time. Soon, you noticed they were laughing at you. Not only laughing but mocking you, imitating your movements, how you picked up a stone, stared at it, lowered your glasses and put it back down. They mocked your glasses, your gestures, your clothes, egging each other on, until all you had to do was frown and they fell about in fits of laughter. Finally you could not take any more. You took your tools and tossed them at their feet.

'You do it,' you said.

Most of the children jumped back, hiding behind

bushes and trees. But one girl came forward. She picked up the hammer. She tapped it against a piece of wood. You took it and showed her how to handle it properly. You thought what it would be simplest to demonstrate, and tried to think of something easy to make. You decided to build a ladder. You needed a ladder, after all, before you could do anything else. So the children stayed and spent the day with you, helping to build a ladder. You showed them which nails to use, which saws. You showed them how to sand the edges.

And that night they must have gone home to tell their parents – the crazy tree-trunk Englishman taught us how to build a ladder – because the next day two men turned up and said, that's it, we're going to help.

My mother laughed, watching your face tell the story while your eyes stayed fixed on the road, the mocking children visible to her as though you had conjured them. Things were different now, you said. Work was under way. Men came every day to work on the house. There was the carpenter whose hands were like plates, the shrewd, gentle roofer, the tiler with fingertips like a gecko who could walk across a beam on his bare feet, and the schoolteacher who never got his hands dirty but sat in his suit smoking and watching all day. You had been demoted, relegated to the job of hod carrier, along with the hard-drinking shepherd, who could not be trusted with a hammer, you were told. In charge of it all was the engineer who had spent twenty years in the navy and so spoke some English and loved to clap you on the back and shake you by the hair at the end of the day. He told you what to pay everybody, but he would take no money for himself. When you tried to give him something, he pushed your hand away in disgust.

My mother watched the valley fold into mountains, purplish-black shapes textured with glinting stones and animals' eyes. She questioned you for details, taking in all the names, the characters, the new words and jobs. Images formed in her mind: a roof made of cypress trees, clay tiles moulded on the thighs of the makers, a house rebuilt from fallen stones in the centuries-old tradition. All the time, the tarmac road was narrowing. Soon it disappeared, fading into a gravelly track. The Avenger's worn-out tyres growled in the rubble but the engine kept pulling. The yellow beams of the headlights barely reached three metres. You might have been driving into a pit of tar. The climb went on and on. My mother watched how carefully you drove, leaning forward, your fingers wrapped around the thin leather steering wheel. Finally the car slowed and stopped, but it wasn't until she heard the jerk of the handbrake that she believed you had arrived.

'That's the cafe,' you said, pointing into the black. 'We're staying in a place just underneath. No one's lived there for decades but it's warm and dry. I'll take you there in a minute. But first come and see the house.'

You left my mother's bags in the car and she followed you down a hill so steep it made her knees ache. She clung to the feeling of your hand wrapped around her wrist. She could hear your breathing and the gentle burr of sleeping chickens. The darkness smelled of goats and sage, milk and warm stone, months turned to days turned to minutes waiting for this. The ground flattened and you veered to the left, then down another sharp hill, shorter and stonier this time.

'This way,' you said.

You guided her up a pile of rocks and stopped. Then you put her hands on what she realised were the arms of a ladder.

The ladder you built, she thought.

'Hold this,' you said.

She watched the shadows of your legs disappear into the darkness. When the swaying-crunching stopped and there was silence, my mother felt her body tense, but she did not feel afraid. It was only the sense of having come so far away from where she had been two days before. Then she heard your voice, calling her up. The ladder was made of rough wood and as she slid her hands upwards she thought of your hands on it, your tools, your plans. The wood seemed to bend with each step. When your hand found her shoulder, she took a breath and realised she had been holding it. You helped her on to a platform made of stones and two creaky planks. As her eyes adjusted, she could make out the shape of the house.

Its rectangular walls were high on the side where they were sitting but collapsed at the opposite end. In the space below their feet she could make out the remains of a floor under a jumble of collapsed beams and below that, a spiky tangle, the mountain. On the one remaining wall were two arched windows, empty of glass, and behind them, a pale light had begun to creep over the mountain edge, illuminating the tree-dense valley and vast plains below. Above, the sky's thick dark was fading too. She felt your eyes on her, watching her take it in. She knew you were waiting for her reaction, and she was trying to find the words for what she felt, pressed inside so much unknown. A dog howled through a chorus of crickets. Your voice was so close she could have touched it.

'What do you think?' you said.

She took a breath. 'It's beautiful.'

In the morning you woke together in the borrowed house, a mattress rolled out across a creaking metal bed frame on the stone floor. My mother stretched and looked around the room she'd seen only by moonlight. There was a stone sink and two wooden chairs beside a fireplace, a metal grate above it and two pots, one small, one large. My mother brushed her hair with her fingers and went to press her face against the round hole in the door. Sunlight burned through the glass. She opened the door and the golden heat licked her ankles. Outside, a vine hung overhead, dappling the concrete, sticky grapes hanging in bunches. She could hear men's voices shouting slightly above, a jagged, rolling argument, and wondered if they were the people she had heard about. When she went back inside, you were dressed already, tidying up. Work started early here, before the heat. What job would she have? Would they let her help? You told her she could certainly help with something.

'Nobody believes what I'm doing here,' you said. 'They don't think it's possible that I'm here to write a poem. There are only three possibilities, they've decided. I'm a smuggler, a madman, or a spy looking for the gold the English dropped in the mountains during the Second World War. Perhaps you can convince them otherwise. Every night in the cafe somebody starts demanding I tell them the truth.'

My mother didn't know what she could do about that. But she did not know the effect she had on people. She did not know how she was.

Within days, it was clear you were right. Everybody loved her, and by association, began to love you. A man with a woman made sense. You were a young couple, out there to start a family, a new life away from cold, expensive England. My mother had a smile for everybody. She chatted to the children and soon their mothers invited her to sit with them on their terraces in the afternoon sun or into their kitchens to sip thick, bitter coffee while they cooked. She tried home-made sausages and fresh feta, hearth-cooked liver and glistening purple olives, working out the language through gestures and guesses. She remembered the names of children, godchildren, grandchildren, cousins and brothers and sisters. She pored over family photos, delighted in the babies placed in her lap. She walked all over the village, right to the top of the mountain to see the tiny, bruised shepherdess, dressed in black for twenty years mourning her only child. She and my mother sat together drinking hot, overproof liquor, exchanging stories that neither and both understood until they had tears in their eyes.

My mother explained you, translated for you and let the children translate for her. She explained no, you weren't married yet, no children either – *yet!* the women's knowing smiles insisted. When they would release her, my mother went to help you with the house, making fresh lemonade or stripping bamboo for the roof. You showed her how, when you stopped at midday, the men tossed salt around, drinking it straight from the shaker.

The summer passed like this. On Sundays, you went to the beach, or drove to the nearest town to eat octopus or souvlaki and chips. My mother had never seen anything like it before – watermelon, calamari, taramasalata, aubergine. You relished watching her eat, could not believe her delight. You talked and drank the local krassi, viscous yellow wine that you called liquid gold, smoked and sat up late in the cafe, eating monkey nuts and sardines, my mother the only woman there. You imagined the house together, the pink marble sink and the arched front door, the balcony that would look out over the mountain. When

September came and she had to go home again, there was no question that your life was now together.

That autumn you returned to London and my mother came to live with you. Then the two of you drove back to Greece together, arriving at Christmas to a house finished in structure only. There were doors, windows and a floor but no water or electricity. For furniture there was a mattress, two wooden chairs and a pile of stones with a flat stone on top for a table. At night you could hear rats running across the floor, dragging anything soft or pliable that had not been secured. They terrified my mother, but you promised they'd disappear once you'd lived there a little longer, along with the scorpions, who had been disturbed by all the moving rocks. You did the plumbing yourself – a sink upstairs and a toilet downstairs that could be reached by a ladder through a square hole cut in the floor.

When the electricity was switched on, you invited everyone in the village to celebrate. There was a party in the house, dancing to bouzouki music on the newly waxed floors, jugs of wine in the sink. The Greeks had laughed at your decision to leave the bamboo lining of the roof uncovered, to put no ceiling in – it was what their grand-parents used to do – so the engineer insisted on hanging a swing from one of the exposed cypress trunks. At the height of the party, the elderly village president sat down on it to make a speech, too tired to stand any longer. He swung gently back and forth, his feet skimming the floor, sipping and spilling his wine as he toasted my mother and you, and declared you official members of the village.

Back in London again, all the two of you wanted was to get back to Greece. But it was hard to find the money, the resources to make a life there possible. You wrote and she taught and it got cold and you argued and you made up and you did not know how you would get back there, and then you did.

And when you did, all of it made sense.

The two of you and the red tiled roof, the thick cypress beams holding it up, the whitewashed walls and the cross above the door, the goat-bell hung on a wire for a doorbell – it was more beautiful than either of you had imagined. A single, long room with a fireplace and sink at one end, a bed and four arched windows at the other. Every time you went back, you added to it, fixed it, built something else that you needed. By 1985 there was a bathroom downstairs, where the animals used to be, with a shower and a smooth stone floor.

In 1986, you got married, and nobody was surprised when the two of you returned the following summer with a baby. A little boy with bright blue eyes like his father. The baby, my brother, was baptised in the village, dipped in oil by the Papas and passed to his godfather, the engineer, who kissed his forehead and wrapped him in white cloth. Returned to my mother, sanctified but distraught, he didn't stop quivering all the way home. The baptism took place the same day as the Panagia festival, so there were tables and chairs delivered to the cafe, souvlaki and beer and dancing until late in the night.

'Your son belongs to the village now,' people kept saying. 'He is baptised here. Why are you leaving? You must come and live here for good.'

That night it was decided – as soon as you got some money together, you would.

A meeting

3 1st January 2014: the day you ended. A date to mirror the other, your birthday, the first day of you. Sebastian Smart Barker, 16th April 1945 to 31st January 2014. That's sixty-eight years, nine months and fifteen days. Eight different decades and fourteen different Prime Ministers. Three wives, two divorces, three daughters, one son. Both parents, a sister and several of your best friends dead. Fourteen books of poetry published and three of essays. One wall of journals full of your meticulous handwriting tracking your thoughts and obsessions since 1962.

> How quickly
> A CV
> Turns into
> An obituary

You wrote. But I don't care about any of that. I am selfish. And devoted to you. I want only the bits that are mine.

I was born on 14th November 1988. The last time I saw you was 29th January 2014.

14th November 1988 to 29th January 2014: the shorter slice of reality during which we coincided.

29th January 2014, two days before you died, around

eleven o'clock in the evening. Through some magical collision of coincidence and intent, it was a proper goodbye, and I'm grateful for it. Though for months afterwards, and kneeling over your body two days later, I could not get over the promise you made me when I left. You said we would have a meeting.

It was January. It was cold. You had been dying for six months. You were tired. We were tired. We were braced for your death any day. I could not sleep because of the nightmares I was having and my boyfriend was avoiding me. I had driven him and most of my friends to despair talking about cancer, mortality, family tensions, all the things you could no longer do.

But there you were in 2014 – still breathing, walking, talking, eating, making plans.

One of the plans was to attend a reading of your poetry in Trinity College Chapel in Cambridge on 29th January. The reading had been arranged months ago – before your diagnosis – and you had thought you would be too ill to go. It would be the second launch of your book *The Land of Gold*. You would read poems from the work alongside two of your friends, also poets, who had organised it, and your wife. It was a religious work and the chapel setting was just right, you said. But it was a literary event, and so you would not be inviting family. We didn't need to be there, you said.

I stewed and my brother rolled his eyes, but our elder sisters – half-sisters – complained. We bloody well did need to be there, they said. Angry emails flew around various family members. The reading was on a Wednesday evening. On Monday afternoon your wife rang me to say she knew it was a bit late, but please would I come. I bought my train tickets as soon as I got off the phone. My sisters already had theirs. My brother said he'd made other plans.

You didn't really want us there, he said. We were space fillers. You wouldn't talk to us.

I wished he hadn't said my fears out loud.

On Wednesday 29th January after work, I met my sisters at Liverpool Street to take the train to Cambridge. We were not together often, the three of us. They were teenagers when my brother and I were born and because our dad left my mum soon after, we rarely saw each other. I was nervous without my brother, a fragment, insufficient proof of us, your second family. When the train pulled into Cambridge, they were going to their hotel and invited me with them. I felt buoyed by this affection and would have liked to go. But I had already asked to see you. And to my surprise, you had said yes.

There was about an hour before we were due to be at the chapel. I walked from the station to Trinity College, where you had booked a room. Your wife let me in before excusing herself – she said she had to finalise some arrangements. You were sitting on the tall wooden bed, your legs stretched over the covers, your hair combed and your suit on, though your suit jacket was hanging on the door. The room was bright and, to my eyes, regal, with its thick carpet and bathroom through an ornate wooden door. The only chair was a large armchair by the window, too heavy to move and too far from you for me to sit in, so I pulled up your wheelchair instead. It had been given to you two months before, when it stopped looking likely you would be given back the power of your legs. There were blankets on it and you told me to keep warm and wrap myself up in them, which I didn't because I was boiling. But I made you laugh admiring how comfortable it was, wheeling myself backwards and forwards with my feet.

After talking about our journeys, the room, the city, the plan for the evening, you said we should get down to business. We had something important to discuss – that was the reason we had given each other, you had given your wife, for the two of us spending this hour together. I was doing some work for you. You had written a long poem on Heidegger. A short section of it had been published in a magazine but you wanted it to exist in print in its entirety. 'Doing the work to get it published is beyond me at this point,' you said. 'That's what you will have to do.' I was responsible for the poem, you said. It was because of me that you had written it. You had talked to both my brother and me about Heidegger as children, translating his ideas into language we could understand, perhaps as a way to understand it yourself. You had been obsessed by him for many years, between your obsessions with Nietzsche and Catholic theology. But when I studied him at university, I discovered completely different ideas to those you had taught us. I sent you the essay I wrote on him, and you said I'd shown you things you never knew. You borrowed the book of his early essays I'd read for my course. You were newly entranced. We talked and wrote to each other about him again. You borrowed my notes. You underlined the words I had written in the margins. And then at last, as was always the result of your scholarly obsessions, you wrote a poem: 'A Treatise on any Model of Being'. 'The title is ironic,' you explained emphatically – it was a poem of questions, an incantatory challenge to the existential philosopher who had questioned everything except the fascist, genocidal policies of his own government. You wanted it to be published but it wasn't ready. You were too old and ill now to do the editing required. You wanted me to do it for you.

You had never trusted me with a task of this magnitude: the responsibility of editing your work, getting it published. I was paralysed with pride and anxiety, certain I would get it wrong. I said I would need some instruction. You said come and see me. I suggested I come before the reading.

So there I was on 29th January at five o'clock, sitting in your wheelchair at the end of your professorial bed, talking about your poem with my make-up on, your smart shoes waiting at the side of the bed.

'You'll know what to do,' you said. 'You can borrow my notes.'

'Will you read it to me?' I said. 'So I can hear it in your voice.'

'What a good idea. Yes. If I can do the reading tonight, I don't see why I shouldn't be able to do that.'

You were worried about the reading because you were so breathless. You had a tumour the size of a tennis ball at the neck of your left lung. The lung had collapsed back in July. There had been an operation and a stent to open it, but it had been slowly crushed again since then. It was hard for you to walk more than a few steps. You were overwhelmed by coughing in the middle of sentences. You said, 'Come over next week and I'll read it to you. You can ask all the questions you like.'

Then you needed to use the bathroom so I helped you out of bed, lending you my arm to walk across the room. I was wearing boots with heels, which I never did, and was two inches or so taller than usual. I am the shortest person in my family, but that evening I towered over you. Where had you gone? It scared me. I stood waiting outside the bathroom door, looking at my legs, my hands, my guilty living body, wishing I'd taken my shoes off at the door.

A short time later, your wife came to take us to the chapel. I helped you into your wheelchair and wrapped you in the blankets until you looked like a fairy-tale king, only your white hair, eyes and fingers poking out. Then

I put all your drugs in my rucksack and pushed you outside, following your wife down the stone paths across the lawns. I pushed you too fast, trying to cancel out the sadness, making sports car sounds and motorbike sounds and jumping up on the back. No longer alone with you, I did not know who to be. Perhaps I felt if I acted like a child, it could be twenty years ago again. You would be young and stronger than me and I would be too young to know one day you wouldn't be. But I tripped on the cobbles and almost tipped you over. You didn't like that. I caught you and apologised, cursing myself because I hadn't seen that however much I wanted there to be, there was nothing light-hearted about this.

Inside the chapel, everything was as I had feared and as my brother had predicted. There were dozens of people who I didn't know and you were whisked off immediately to greet them and have your microphone fitted. I looked around for someone I recognised. Most of the crowd were around your age, academics and poets with white hair and bedraggled suits.

The group of people nearest me opened up and a man with a green suit and a smile that spread all over his face turned to me and said, 'Hello! Welcome.' He introduced himself as one of the professors here. 'And what brought you along?' he said.

'I'm here for the reading.'

'Oh, that's great. Are you a Trinity student?'

'No, my dad is reading.'

He frowned. 'Your dad?'

'Sebastian Barker.'

I watched his expression change as he realised he was not talking to a curious undergraduate but a woman on the brink of her father's death. He looked over his shoulder to where my sisters were standing and I understood his confusion. He had already met Sebastian's daughters.

'I didn't know he had a daughter so young,' he said.

'I'm twenty-five.'

'Oh!'

I felt sorry for him then, how awkward he looked. All these mistakes in a professor were uncouth. It was uncomfortable to be so troubling to someone. It was uncomfortable to watch him calculate my grief. Perhaps he felt the same, because he questioned me then as he might have any student, asking me about the poets and authors I was into, what I had studied, what I did for work. He was outraged I had not read Proust, who he felt was the greatest writer ever to have lived, while I stood there worrying that I still had all your drugs in my bag. What if you needed them during the reading? What if you started coughing and couldn't stop? What if you died on the altar in front of all of us and I couldn't get close enough to say goodbye and this man was still talking about Proust?

Somebody cleared their throat and the conversation died down. We were being called in. People filed into the pews arranged along either side of the chapel, perpendicular to the altar where you were sitting with the other readers and your wife. They were in chairs while you were in your wheelchair. One of the organisers was standing waving people into their seats.

The hubbub of people arranging themselves faded and the lights were turned down. One of your poet friends introduced you and the others and the book. He compared your lyric poetry to Blake's in its 'simplicity and purity', tracing your Greek poems to Odysseus Elytis, Giorgios Seferis, the fifteen-syllable line of Greek folk poetry, 'all the way back to the Byzantine Bible'. His voice was excited, serious, checking back towards you every now and then with a look somewhere between affection and curiosity. He said something about your family, your poet father and poet mother, your poet wife. You watched him with an intensity that troubled me. 'How quickly/ A CV / Turns into/ An obituary.' Had he written yours already? His voice echoed, ghostly in the cold, stony space, the lights low and yellow and flickering.

Your face.

Your hands holding your marked copy of the book.

Your blue suit loose and slightly crumpled.

Your grey-white combed hair.

Your frown and your gaze fixed on the speaker.

The way your wheelchair was slightly lower than the chairs the others were sitting on.

The way this small fact was what hurt the most: not

that you were in a wheelchair, but that it had been arranged so that the audience must stare at the meaning of this. You were leaving us behind already. You had already shifted part of the way into another plane.

As though to underline this further, we could hear your breath over the mic. You were the only one with a microphone, so your faltering breath was projected across the chapel. We heard every crack in it, every strain of your lungs. We heard the things you whispered to yourself. 'I don't know what the collective noun is for poets,' the chaplain said, introducing the event. 'Gaggle,' you said under your crackling breath, a tiny laugh, '. . . giggle.'

The reading began.

Your wife read first. Then your friends, then your wife again, your breath beneath their words throughout. They read in their poet voices, confident and professional and clear, their healthy lungs pushing healthy breath into words made from your life. It gave me the same feeling as when I towered over you on the way to the bathroom. I was impatient. I wanted you to read. The first reader again. He read the poem you wrote for me, 'Scorpio Rising', breathing his own meaning into it, so far from the one I heard there, and I thought that he knew nothing, not one scrap of what had happened between us to allow you to write those words. That poem you had first written as a text message, which you'd sent to me from Greece in the middle of the night, the first year you owned a mobile phone. It was a decade ago, but I could still remember receiving it, still see the words on the greenish pixellated screen.

And then it was your turn to read.

Your voice.

Shaking.

Your shaking voice.

Your gravitas voice.

Your reading voice.

Your voice always shook when you read, but tonight that shaking had a new meaning.

I wondered if you had taken beta blockers. You got stage fright and had taken them for years to combat it. You never read without them. But I didn't know if you had needed them tonight. If there was anything left you were afraid of.

You were reading your sequence of tiny poems, 'Ten Zonulets'. You paused from reading to explain what a zonulet was: 'A little zone,' you said. You loved that word, I knew, because you had explained it to me enough times to annoy me over the past couple of years.

Next you read 'The Ballad of True Regret' – 'Never to look on the clouds again, / Never the flowers, nor seas'. The lines all rolling together. Those images – the things you found sweet in life, things to live for, things you didn't want to lose – and the strength in your voice, and all the things you knew that we didn't. We could not know what it was for you and yet you were asking us to imagine, your poem was asking us to imagine, the feeling, the simple fact *you will not be here*. You will be nowhere. You would be nowhere. All of us, one day, would be nowhere.

After you finished that poem your breath on the mic was unbearable. You could not catch it. You were behind it, gasping, your voice distorted. We could hear your chest working. I felt it in my own chest – your diaphragm moving up and down, pulling in the cold chapel air – all of us made aware of this damp place, this uncomfortable place, so obviously funereal, the echoes and shadows as though death had already come. I wanted anyone to read then, anyone's voice to drown out the sound of your shallow breath.

It went on for an hour in the flickering light, all of us transfixed and some bewildered, the yellow making your pale eyes glint. Afterwards, the reader who had introduced you asked the audience for questions. Someone took a microphone around. The questioners' voices sounded far away, as though they were speaking from above the ocean while everybody listening was with you and your wheezing lungs on the sea floor below. It was only you responding to the questions, and the demand of speaking strained your lungs and we could hear it – the questions taking your life force breath by breath. There were questions from students, from other poets, from friends. My sisters asked questions about parts of the poems they recognised – the nights you spent drinking diluted wine on the beach in Greece while they danced in the nearby 'discotheque'.

Answering those questions you were the person I remembered from years ago.

You said, 'How do you get the purple glow of the dance floor into a theological poem?'

You said, 'You have to let yourself be certain that what you are writing is what you actually meant, not what you were nudging yourself to mean or hoping someone else would be satisfied by. You've got to be satisfied yourself.'

You said, 'You mustn't make me laugh, because I can't—'

You said, 'I was out for a walk, no intention of writing a poem, when the mountains ceased to be mountains and started to become a living presence that was anything but benign. I don't think they saw any reason they should be benign, these darn great huge things, it was just like the sea except it was rock and it was coming towards me. I just hoped I would get it all down and get away in one piece.'

You said, 'Well, my other daughter will remember the Land of Gold is the setting of a children's book I wrote . . .'

You said that and you looked right at me. I beamed back. Of course I remembered. I remembered everything – 'The Land of Gold' and those devouring mountains, the laughter in your voice and how important it was for you that a poem, a piece of work, was what it was, not what you wanted it to be. I didn't care about anything then – the other poets with their booming voices, the way your wheelchair was too low, the people who didn't know you had a third daughter, the certainty I would not get to speak to you after. You remembered me. You looked right at me. You knew who I was.

The formalities ended and were followed by the drinks reception: all those hushed, bright voices discussing your strength and courage, your sense of humour. You signed books and gestured with your glass of wine from your wheelchair, looking like so many old poets who'd gone before you, who I'd seen do just that over the years on the rare occasions you invited us to such events. Your scarves and blankets were forgotten, hanging from the arms of the chair. I stood at the edge and tried to avoid any more conversations about literature. Then guests were ushered out, leaving only the organisers, your family and theirs, a couple of close friends. We were going for dinner at a nearby restaurant. You asked if I was coming or if I had to catch my train.

'Of course I'm coming,' I said.

The dark January streets, cobbled and winding. The blue-black sky, no drizzle, not even damp. It was a dry, clear night and there was a dozen or so of us – a gaggle or a giggle of poets and academics and daughters, released from the sepulchral chapel and slightly drunk. There was a long table prepared in the restaurant and I pushed your chair up to the middle of it. My sisters sat beside and opposite you, your wife on the other side. The poets who had read alongside you were close by too, plus the organisers. I sat a few people away, beside a woman who was married to a friend of yours who couldn't be there. She was candid and gentle and I liked her immediately, and we spoke for most of the dinner. She asked about my mother and I loved her for that. And she was not afraid to mention the fact you were going to die.

In my memory, you are drinking and gesticulating, nodding and shaking your head throughout. Was there food? Did we eat it? Who were all the other people? My cheeks were burning with the heat, the wine, my own shyness. People were asking you about your work, the house you built in Greece where the mountains came to life. You asked for the bottle of morphine from my bag and I gave it to you. That is the most definite image I have of you – a glass of red wine in one hand, a bottle of morphine in the other, necking both, your eyes glittering, laughing your way through all this serious talk. You were teasing everybody with your cryptic answers, the same way you had always teased me. Laughter had never been frivolous for you but the gravest way to respond.

You were a giggle of a poet, blind drunk on what had been possible in life. All the things you wanted that you had never got, and all the greater, unexpected things that had arrived in their wake.

Later on, several people had left and there were empty seats at the table. My sisters had left. Your wife had swapped places to speak to someone else. I got up to go to the bathroom and when I came back, you asked where I'd been. A woman leaning across the empty chair beside you said, 'It's time you sat here, isn't it?'

I sat down. You poured me a glass of wine. I was your guest, then, daughter-guest, a stranger to these people and they strangers to me. You carried on talking to the woman, to your friends, and I tried not to look so pleased about the small fact of being close to you.

My mum says that when you used to go to parties and George Barker, your own poet-father, was there, everybody would take turns sitting next to him, talking to him. She says that you would have to wait your turn too. It had always sounded to me a little sad, waiting for your turn to sit beside your own dad, but tonight I realised I didn't mind at all. You almost knocked over the bottle of morphine and frowned, handed it to me, fumbling with the lid, saying, 'You better put this somewhere safe.' I put it back in my rucksack and you poured yourself another glass of wine.

It was half past ten and then it was almost eleven. The last train back to London was at eleven thirty. Some of your friends had promised me a lift to the station. They were gathering their things, saying goodbye. I didn't want to leave you. But I had to get back to London. I had nowhere to stay, work tomorrow. I held my rucksack on my lap.

I said, 'Daddy, I'll ring you tomorrow.'

You said, 'Yes, we need to talk about the treatise.'

I said, 'I'll come over next week and we can talk about it.'

'Absolutely,' you said. 'We'll have a meeting.'

'We better go,' someone said – there were three of them waiting for me.

'I love you,' I said, quiet as I could, afraid of so many ears.

'I love you too!' you almost shouted, sipping your wine and announcing it to the table. 'This is my daughter,' you announced. 'She got a first-class degree in philosophy!'

I stared at the floor, my face burning. Then you hugged me, the kind of jostling hug you were known for, warm and tough at the same time, your glass still raised over my shoulder. 'We'll have a meeting,' you said.

I put on my coat and waved at the others, hugged your wife and went out.

It had started to rain. I sat in the back of the car and listened to your friends talking. I watched through the window, the wet street flashing in the car lights. The station appeared. I started to say goodbye and someone saw the time and told me to run. I ran, the doors closing seconds behind me. The carriage was empty and I sat down in my coat. I sat with the hood up, my scarf wrapped around my face, my rucksack clutched on my lap, watching the city lights get sparser until they faded to greeny-black fields and hedges.

I didn't read. I didn't look at my phone. I didn't bite my nails or undo my coat. I sat there, watching the countryside overlaid with the evening, all the things that had happened that it was hard to believe.

Just after Welwyn Garden City I remembered your drugs. I opened my bag and there they were – three white boxes of pills and two dark glass bottles of morphine. I'd taken everything. I rang you in a panic but you didn't answer. I texted you. I hoped you were right about how useless they were.

From Liverpool Street, I took the Tube back to Holloway and walked home in a trance, my face slick with drizzle. Inside, I took off my wet clothes and brushed my teeth and checked my phone. You still hadn't replied. I got into bed and fell asleep, the wine and the warmth after the cold and the endless parade of feelings knocking me out.

I woke up. I went to work. You texted me, saying only 'Bon jour mon amour' and nothing about the drugs. I didn't ring you. I assumed you wanted to rest.

I met my boyfriend after work. He made me dinner and let me talk about the evening. It was still so much inside me, there was no room for anything else. I said to him, sitting cross-legged on his bed last thing that night, 'I just don't think it could be possible for him to die. He's too many people. He needs to be alive so they can all exist in one place.' We brushed our teeth and went to sleep.

In the morning, I was woken by a nightmare. You and I had gone to Greece and hired a car. We were driving along a dusty track. It was long, narrow and winding, precipices on either side. You were driving but you said it was my turn. I said I couldn't, I didn't know how. You insisted. I pleaded with you. You slid out of the seat and forced me to take the wheel. I tried, but I couldn't control it. The road was too thin. I drove us off the mountain.

That's what woke me up – the swerve, the fall, the certainty we'd die. My heart was racing. I could still see it all – the gaping valley, you sitting beside me. I replayed it in my head. The burnt-orange road and your insistence, my reluctance, my mistake. I was awake but my eyes were closed. The bed was empty – my boyfriend had already got up. I opened my eyes and reached for my phone to check the time. I pressed the button to light the screen. Underneath the large numbers that read 07:15, a green banner said I had four missed calls. They were all from your wife.

Four missed calls, starting at 06:32.

06:36. 06:48. 06:52.

She had left two voicemails. I pressed the button to hear them.

Her voice. Her panic. Voices I didn't recognise in the background, counting.

I pressed another button to ring her. She answered straight away. There were no background noises now. She told me what I already knew. And yet to me in that moment the world fell away, leaving a completely new one in its place.

'Where is he?' I said.

You were at home – your body was at home. The paramedics had just left. I said I would call a taxi.

What happened then?

It took so long to arrive. My boyfriend lent me the cash for it. I waited shaking on his bedroom floor. I picked up my brother on the way. He asked the driver to turn off the radio playing 1980s power ballads. We got to the house. There were police in the living room. Protocol, they explained, because you died at home. Your wife said you were upstairs and we went straight up to see you. You were lying on the floor beside the bed, what looked like a curtain draped across you, a plastic tube taped in your mouth. I knelt down beside you. My brother knelt at your feet. I had never seen a dead body before.

And all the same, I did not believe it. I stroked the hair from your forehead and your skin was still warm. I kissed your face. I held your left hand, your other hand in my brother's. But there was only one thing I was thinking about. The words kept running around my head. When my brother had gone from the room, I stayed behind, whispering them to you.

'You said we would have a meeting.'

If I insisted, if I said the words enough, perhaps you would remember. Perhaps you would sit up and say yes, you hadn't forgotten, you would come.

I waited all day.

The police left just after we got there. A few minutes later, my sisters arrived, followed by my mother.

My mother had been in that house just once before, to say goodbye to you a few weeks earlier. She only came today, she said, for my brother and me. But she moved between the rooms, between the cracks in our mismatched family, with a grace and sensitivity that filled me with awe, though there were moments when I could feel what it cost her.

At some point, your priest arrived and took us up in turns to pray with your body. My brother and I knelt beside you again, whispering words our maternal grandmother had taught us. After, the priest said there was nothing to be sad about because you had gone where you most wanted to be. Then he left and the rest of us sat together in the front room, staring between our phones and the carpet, a collection of relatives more like acquaintances, both united and estranged by loss, waiting for your GP. More protocol: the undertakers couldn't come to collect you until your GP had signed off the cause of death. He was stuck in traffic on the A1.

I checked on you every hour. I said I was going to the toilet and snuck back into your room. I was surprised, and surprised at my surprise, to find you still lying there. I spoke to you, let my eyes absorb the patterns of you in a way that had never been possible while you were alive.

I said, 'Daddy? Daddy. Get up. Come on.'

It seemed so obvious to me that you would do. It seemed so obvious to me that it would do, when out of the corner of my eye I saw your chest moving. I jumped up, ready to run downstairs and tell everybody. But I stared harder and could not be sure it moved again.

Your forehead was getting colder.

It was ten o'clock, eleven, almost twelve.

The GP had turned off the A1.

The six of us remained in the living room, our private griefs evolving. People made attempts at talking. I was afraid to look at anyone else. Once, when I stared at my knees to avoid the eyes of the conversation, I felt the hugeness of your hand warm the back of my head. A shot of joy surged through me and I really had to leave the room then.

Just before one o'clock, the GP arrived. He signed the forms he needed to sign and said things some of us found comforting. People talked about 'a good death'. Then my sister made the call and the undertakers said they would be there in half an hour. I went up to see you again.

'Daddy?' I said.

The undertakers came and I thought they were lying. They took you away and I thought, They're in for a shock.

I waited that night for the call.

I waited for weeks and months. I waited all through 2014. I was used to waiting for you. It was familiar. You had returned so many times from being gone forever. There were promises you kept, and promises you didn't, but I couldn't shake the certainty you'd keep this one, however long it took.

We would have a meeting.

A Viennetta and a Chinese takeaway

Your diagnosis, once it was given, was uncomplicated. A single word to explain the collection of symptoms you had been experiencing for over six months.

The first and most innocuous symptom: you'd lost weight – that was something that pleased you. You had been told to lose weight repeatedly by doctors, but had never tried to and so never succeeded. You had been steadily gaining weight, instead, and had seen no problem with that. But now you were smug about your surprise weight loss, in the way you were smug about so many things, charmingly so, immune to the prosaic trials of other people's lives. You hadn't followed the recommendations for exercise, the suggestions to join a gym or community fitness initiatives. You found them absurd. '"Exercise" they call it,' you said. 'Well, walking is what I do. They want you to do all these crazy things but walking is the best exercise of all.'

Then the following spring you started to cough. You had a cold, flu, a chest infection, bronchitis – you kept changing your mind about the cause. You didn't need to see a doctor, you said. It was just a cough. But when I heard you'd had the same cough for three months, I pleaded with you to make an appointment. You went to your GP. Your GP sent you for a scan. The scan showed nothing unusual. You were smug about that too: I'd been wrong, hypochondriac, it was just a cough, the winter, a cold, the last dregs of flu, that was all. You continued to cough and drink cough medicine. Then on 2nd July, mid-afternoon, you found yourself unable to breathe. You went to A&E. Your left lung had collapsed. For a short time you were quarantined on the possibility you might have tuberculosis. You were sent for another scan, the same kind you'd had three weeks before, which supposedly showed nothing. This time it did not show nothing. This time it showed a mass in your left lung. The doctors and nurses used the word 'mass' for twenty-four hours while the biopsy was done and then they started using the word 'tumour'.

I visited you before the mass had become a tumour. You were in Homerton Hospital, still in quarantine, doing an excellent job acting the part of a tuberculosis patient. Anachronism suited you. I sat by your bed and held your hand. Nobody else was there. I had received a call the evening before on my way home from a late shift. It was your wife. She never rang me, so I knew it was bad news. Besides, it was almost midnight.

'Sebastian's lung has collapsed,' she said.

What did that mean?

There were several reasons. She told me it could be tuberculosis. She told me the name of the ward. I said I would visit tomorrow. After we'd hung up, I googled it:

collapsed lung. Pneumothorax. It was what happened when someone was stabbed.

It was now tomorrow and I was sitting there beside you. We talked about the breathlessness you had felt just before it happened, how all of a sudden your chest became tight. You said you'd almost fallen but managed to sit down and your wife had called an ambulance. They brought you here. Understandably, you were subdued. You were wearing a paper mask. You couldn't walk far. You were a big man and one lung could not provide enough oxygen. You had already spent months unable to walk, after you had your hip replaced the previous summer. You had already spent months in hospital, too, because your new hip got infected.

You hated being in hospital, but you had your ways of making it bearable. For example, befriending the nurses. The present nurse's name was Sunny. When she came in you told me that her name was just right, she was just like a sunny day, and she laughed. I asked her to explain to me what had happened, what treatment you'd had and what tests had been done. You encouraged me to ask her because you hadn't understood it yourself, you said. You were on strong painkillers as well as morphine for the breathlessness. The nurse explained to me what they had found, calling it a mass, and I asked if that meant it was not tuberculosis. She said yes, almost certainly. I asked if that meant you could take off the mask. She looked unsure but agreed. You took it off.

When Sunny had gone and we were alone again, we began to talk with the ease that had arisen between us over the past year. There was an openness and familiarity that several events had created. After your hip replacement, I had visited you in hospital and at home almost every day. A few months after that, you helped me move house following a difficult break-up. A short time after this – perhaps because of this – we had an argument. Bolstered by our new intimacy, I did not drop the issue, either. I explained what had happened, why it hurt me, why I didn't want to see you. You sent me emails, text messages, voicemails and I ignored them. I can't say that I didn't enjoy this, how our roles had become reversed, that I didn't relish small feelings of vengeance against you – you who had always left me. It was months before I saw you again. You left me a voicemail saying you'd had a dream that I came to see you. I could hear it in your voice, the dream, the emotion, and it is painful still to remember. I knew that feeling. I knew those dreams. I gave in and rang you and we met the next day.

That was when I heard about your cough, your chest infection. That was when I heard you hadn't seen a doctor. That was when I pleaded with you to see one.

You promised me you would, 'If only to please you.'

What were we arguing about? Something so minor, I wish I didn't remember.

A new hip, a break-up, an argument, a promise – these four things together meant we were no longer who we had been. There could be no pretence any more of being infallible, and though we would not have put this into words, it felt to me like there was a new bond between us, more imperfect and yet therefore sturdier than before. So I sat in the chair beside your bed talking to you with ease, making you laugh and answering your questions truthfully, while all the time the word 'mass' flickered and turned in my head.

Your wife arrived with food for you and I chatted to the two of you for a while before leaving. I made you both promise to ring me straight away if there was any news, though I felt doubtful that you would. The new bond did not extend to including me in your everyday life. I went home.

I had just started seeing someone who I was tentatively calling my boyfriend, and the next night he was cooking a fancy dinner for his housemates. They had a Wednesday-night dinner rota, which, to a bunch of recent graduates, seemed the height of sophistication. My boyfriend liked cooking and was keen to impress his friends. It was unheard of, he said, for anyone else to be invited. I should feel honoured. I told him I would bring a Viennetta.

I happened to be working close to his house that day, and when I had finished, I walked up Holloway Road to Morrisons to buy one. It was 3rd July, the beginning of a heatwave. I was hot and vaguely happy, worried about you, but not overly so. I had not heard from you or your wife all day. I had my phone in my hand, waiting for your call. I'd tried ringing but the line was engaged.

So it happened that the moment I learned you had lung cancer, I was in the fruit section of the Morrisons on Holloway Road, staring at the apples that happened to be in the only section where I could get signal, nodding and taking in the words – 'mass' meant 'tumour', the mass was a tumour, the size of a tennis ball, right next to the heart – they would learn more next week after a biopsy, more scans, more tests and talks with consultants. For now you would be going home to rest in bed – no you were feeling all right, yes fine, but you had better go and ring somebody else.

Lung cancer.

Apples.

Viennetta.

'Excuse me?'

I blinked at a woman with a trolley and a child several times before I understood and stepped out of the way.

I stared at my phone and wondered what I was supposed to do. What did it mean to buy a Viennetta after finding out your dad has cancer? I rang my mum and then my brother and neither answered. I brought up my new boyfriend's number but could not think what I would say to him. I thought that it didn't make sense not to buy the Viennetta, that if I didn't buy it, there would be nothing for after his meal and perhaps someone else would have to go to the shop. Whether or not I bought a Viennetta, you would still have cancer. I found the freezer section and chose a Viennetta. The cold cuboid was slimy with condensation. I paid for it and put it in my rucksack. I walked the ten minutes to the house, trying but unable to figure out what would be different now, what had changed about the world, what would happen, what I should do.

My boyfriend answered the door in such an obviously good mood that I was startled.

He hugged me. Then his expression changed as he took in my demeanour. 'Are you all right?' he said.

I looked at him, trying to work out what to say. The words still sounded improbable to me. Melodramatic, almost, like bad TV. But I couldn't think of any other way.

'My dad has cancer,' I said.

He hugged me again, harder this time, crushing my nose against his ribs. I bit my cheek, feeling dizzy and slightly oppressed, unable to think, but grateful. He was not entirely unprepared, perhaps, because he had been with me two nights before when I got the call from your wife. But I didn't know him well. More importantly, he didn't know you at all.

I followed him into the kitchen and gave him the Viennetta to put in the freezer. There were a dozen tiny white bowls lined up on the counter beside the hob. He had prepared all the ingredients ready to tip into the pan. It looked so neat, I thought, like a cooking show. Beside the bowls was a large tray with filo pastry unrolled across it. Everything in the room was clean and precise and bright with the early evening sunlight and I wanted to be there, did not want to go home and sit alone with your cancer, but I felt peculiar and afraid and embarrassed, confused by it all. I did not know where I should be. I did not know how neatly arranged white bowls of prepared ingredients fitted with cancer. I did not know how cleanliness, dinner parties, new boyfriends fitted with diagnoses of critical illnesses. I teased my boyfriend for his line-up of bowls and he laughed uneasily and made a show of explaining the process to me and then my phone rang and it was my mum.

I told her the news. She was calmer than I anticipated, taking in this information and asking questions as though she had done all this before.

As though she had – of course she had. It was only that I had been able to ignore it. All these things a person is too young to know until all at once youth is irrelevant, a disguise for plain ignorance. The line between 'I just can't imagine' and cruel familiarity is flimsy and self-prescribed. My mum's mum had died of cancer a decade earlier, her dad of a heart attack a decade before that, her best friend, also of cancer, sometime in between. On top of this she is a psychotherapist; she listens to people's sadnesses all day long. It was easy to imagine the powerful presence she might provide in her working life.

'He'll be taken good care of now, Xanthi,' she said. 'They won't let him be in any pain.'

Any pain.

I was standing at the sink in my new boyfriend's bathroom but I might have been anywhere. In the mirror my face looked smudged, like it wasn't really there. I tried to tune into my mum's voice, her low, soft voice, and though I could not understand all the words, by her tone she made them mean something real and good. It was as though she put my skin back on, set my bones back in the right place.

We ate the meal. We ate the Viennetta. I did not mention you. Everyone was loud and irreverent, making fun of each other – a bunch of twenty-four-year-olds at ease in the summer evening. Afterwards, they watched Bear Grylls' new survival show, and I watched them watching it, watched myself, troubled by the incoherence of things.

I rang you again before I went to sleep and you said you were going home the next day. I said I would come and see you.

I did come and see you. I have a photo of you from that evening. You look older than in any other photo I have of you, older than you did later on. You are sitting in an armchair, tea towels spread over your knees and tucked into the neck of your shirt, a plate of egg fried rice, lemon chicken and crispy seaweed on your lap. You are resting your elbows on the high arms of the chair, holding up your knife and fork, and you are looking at me with a kind of animal bewilderment that should never have been captured in a photo. You were nauseous from the drugs you had been given and had requested a Chinese takeaway as something you could eat. I'd never known you liked Chinese takeaways, would not have guessed you knew how to get one. I was intrigued to hear what you ordered – all the same things we used to get with my mum.

I sat with you while you ate. It was hard for you to talk. The hospital hadn't been able to reinflate your lung. It wouldn't be possible to do so without a major operation. Most movements left you breathless. But you said that you were happy to have me sitting there while you ate, and I was happy to be there, watching you, your hair unwashed and curling up behind your ears, silvery stubble from several days without the chance to shave.

A Viennetta.

A row of small white bowls.

My mum's voice on the phone.

A Chinese takeaway.

Your delight in two triangles of sesame toast.

A meal eaten off tea towels.

A meal with strangers I was trying to impress.

A phone call in a supermarket.

The banal necessity of eating.

These things seemed so extraordinary to me then, so particular, as though themselves symptomatic of cancer.

Was this the new life we had fallen into, absurd and

prosaic at the same time? Shouldn't a cancer diagnosis come with a thunderstorm, lightning and earthquakes, extravagant feasts or extravagant fasting? Shouldn't it come with a manual?

I needed a manual. I learned everything too late.

'Daddy, did they not tell you anything yet? I mean what did they tell you, you know, about your illness?'

You looked at me over your forkful of rice and seaweed. Your eyes were sharp and cold. You said, 'Xanthi, you can call it cancer.'

SSB's Dictionary

Trout-tickling: agreeing with someone whose views you find offensive in order to draw out their perspective with the aim of demonstrating their illogic or malevolence, either to the speaker themselves or to anyone listening. From the method used to catch trout whereby the fisherman tickles the belly of the fish to put it into a trance before grabbing it out of the water.

16th April 2014

My flatmate talking about her work friend leaving: 'It's just so sad thinking someone won't be in your life any more.'

Yeah? I think. You tell me.

It's my dad's birthday and he's not here and neither are the months between us. I mean March – where was March? I don't remember March at all.

All I want all week is to go and see him. Brain says, 'Well, it's not great weather for cycling all the way to Manor Park and sitting in cemeteries,' but that's not what I meant. I don't want a cemetery. I want to cycle over to his house, let myself in, down a glass of water, climb the stairs and hear him calling, *Xanthi? Xanthi?* with that inflection of delight. His face bright against the cream walls, shirt all faded, Kyparissia Beach T-shirt showing through. Always so smart, he didn't live old enough not to be smart.

I look at crumbling old men all the time, thinking, Daddy, would you have wanted to be so old?

I want to hug him, and then go back downstairs to make him a sandwich.

Instead I go for a walk with my mum and brother, talk about anything but him. When I say that I miss him, my brother says, 'Well, I miss my globe!' He means the one our dad gave him which I've nicked and put in my room. He means objects warrant more feeling than the man. He means he doesn't want to talk about our dad. My mum will talk but her eyes go to places I can't know.

A woman I work for says, 'It must be so hard for your mother.'

I think, You have no idea.

I have to stop thinking he's not dead because he is. He is dead.

No I don't believe it. Words have no purchase. Maybe he will call me up tomorrow. No idea what I mean. The meaning weighs nothing. He said it was impossible. Something cannot become nothing. And still he touches the back of my head, maybe that's why it's so hot. I think how well I know the pressure of that hand, how it held my hand when I was small so tightly that it hurt, a deep ache, I had to tug his hand open every few minutes and wiggle my crushed fingers to stop the pins and needles.

On the way back from the park I forget to speak but when I get home I've chewed my fingertips to a shiny translucent red.

I realised I don't know what dead means. I say, *Daddy?* and he says, *Yep?*

There's something very wrong with me. The other day I checked my phone and a little green box said I had one missed call and a voicemail from him. There you go, I thought, I was right. I pressed it, ready for proof. Of course it wasn't him. The house phone number, saved with only his name. But for a moment I could not doubt it.

Revolting sound of wanting. Hollow scooped hole in the neck, throat, chest.

One minute I'm full of light and disbelief, the next minute I'm sad as hell. Like last night. I couldn't think of anything to say and then I couldn't breathe; my lungs closed up, and I coughed every time I tried to take a breath. My friend sat there painting and repainting her nails in the silence until I drank enough rum that the words spilled out.

She said, 'You can't stop thinking about him, can you?'

I said, 'That's the problem, he's in my head all the time, I see him in every tiny thing I do.'

My friend said, 'That's okay, though, that's okay.'

But she doesn't know what it's like to watch face after face shrink from you, wincing. I emptied a table at the pub the other day, scared two men off the sofa at my boyfriend's house. At work I'm sure the children can see the Grim Reaper hovering behind the desk. Last Tuesday I got so paranoid I cancelled all my lessons, thinking I would do something bright and constructive, then spent the afternoon lying on the floor listening to the CD of him reading his poem on repeat. Now his voice is always on in the background and when I look in the mirror it's not my face it's his.

'You miss him,' she said.

I try to explain that's not the point. It's the fact that I

thought it would end but it doesn't. It only gets faster and faster.

The man in the car telling me he didn't want children. And the man in blue Levi's, red shirt tucked in, picking me up from school for the first time. He was late. I was the last one, or almost. Teacher about to usher us inside. But he marched around the playground gates like some kind of cowboy, his hand in his back pocket ready to draw a gun for me. His car had been smashed up. A truck wasn't looking and drove into him. We inspected the damage. The boot crumpled like a piece of paper. It looked alive. Biological. And he told me how the way the metal crunched, the malleability of the material, saved him by killing the car. Still, his invincible hands drove us in it back to his flat, where he sat me on the counter to eat Marmite on toast before showing me his oil paintings, still drying from earlier that day. His flat was a mythological cave to me, smelling like turpentine and dust and the leather of his black sofa, the manuscripts of his long poem tied in a metre-long bundle on the top shelf.

I thought:

My daddy is a genius. His brain is the scale of mountains.

Where am I?

I love him.

He writes books. My daddy is a poet.

No, I don't live with him.

My daddy is picking me up today.

But that is twenty-one years ago.

SSB's Dictionary

Dirty old rag: an old piece of cloth kept for general use, including cleaning cars, drying hands, polishing found objects, rubbing beeswax into wood, etc. Not necessarily dirty but always old.

Gifts

You went away for at least four months of the year. Sometimes alone and sometimes with your wife. She was a writer as well as a teacher and when it was the school holidays, she liked to get out of the city to as remote a place as possible, places she couldn't be reached. Places you couldn't be reached. You would disappear for months and our mother would rail against you but when you came back, we were always excited to see what presents you'd brought. Giant Toblerones were usually included, along with leathery boxes, carved wooden ornaments, key rings. Sometimes you brought me jewellery – a pearly moon necklace, a smooth blue opal on a silver chain. I liked those. Though I had no other jewellery and would have sworn I wasn't interested in it, whatever you brought me I would put on and refuse to take off no matter how many uniform penalties I got.

But whatever you brought us, accompanying these gifts there would always be knives. At first it was penknives, the classic Swiss Army Knife in red with its flick-out scissors and mini saw. Later you moved on to hunting knives with carved wooden handles, inlayed with precious stones. My brother and I both had substantial collections by the time we were teenagers, the blades engraved with our names in curlicue. I got the small

ones, colourful and sharp; my brother the giant multi-
bladed ones. My brother caught me in the eyelid with his
first, then severed the top of his thumb with another. I
still have the scar and so does he.

One summer you made us slingshots out of wood you
found on the canal down by Camden Lock, two perfect
Y-shaped branches. You dried and stripped the wood,
sanding the grain until it was yellowish and creamy
smooth. They smelled like beeswax, the insides of trees,
your hands, and you took us to see the cobbler on
Gaisford Street – a tiny man, hunched and cobbled on
the face with sunken, expectant eyes – to ask for leather
for the shots. He gave us two oval scraps in royal blue,
smooth on one side and rough on the other, the inside
and outside of a cow. You explained the project and he
refused to charge us. We found elastic in my mother's
sewing box.

'You'll have someone's eye out. What on earth was
he thinking?'

Her sigh cascading between thwacks of elastic, the
scatter of pebbles fired into dirt. The elastic was loose,
making it hard to aim. We tried, but we never got closer
than a shoulder, a sting on the hip, until my brother took
to using his as a club and whacked me over the head.

Another time you made us bows and arrows. More
perfectly shaped wood found during your afternoon
walks along the canal, you said, this time through
Hackney marshes. Long, thin, flexible sticks for the bows,

stripped and sanded to give an even arc; twigs whittled to sharp points for the arrows, the blunt ends spliced with pigeon feathers and circled red for mine, blue for my brother's. The quills were cardboard tubes covered in brown tape and paper, our initials inked in fountain pen, the same pen that wrote our full names in tiny capitals along the bows. There was a hum to the string when we pulled it taut, aiming fingers, elbow, shoulder, nose, eye.

'Zen and the art of archery,' you said. 'Become the arrow. Don't think.'

Then my brother got one in his upper arm. The thrill of it – my brother's yelp, the blood and plasters, my mother's face that night.

Wednesday nights, for a year or so, you yourself were the gift – you babysat. While my mother began training as a counsellor, in search of a new life, you cooked us fish fingers and chips in her flat. You were too big for the kitchen, malcoordinated with pans and cutlery, a prized sight in the domestic space, our home you'd always been a hole in. This was the second place we lived without you. I don't remember you beyond the doorway of the first.

We ate our dinner, splashed the ketchup, wiped our fingers on our knees. Fish fingers fried black and crispy, not bright orange, baked like our mother made. You had some too. Then you sat in the armchair she had re-covered, a hand-me-down-and-down-and-down, pulled square in front of the TV. The chair had two flat arms and my brother and I took one each, sitting closer than we would have with our mother because you were always so huge and far away. You were huge like an oak tree, exactly the kind we wanted to climb on. Huger, I thought, than all the other possible dads who came and went. You used to let me rub my cheeks on your sharp stubble, 'Like a puppy,' you said, 'cleaning herself.'

We watched *How Do They Do That?* and after, you'd talk us through all the inventions, the possibilities of science and technology, the human mind. You wanted us to know exactly how things worked – but if there was no explanation, all the better. You were as amazed as we were by the man who remembered the name and hometown of all 2,000 audience members. You could not take your eyes off him.

Do you remember what it felt like, having us sitting one on each knee?

Do you remember the night I am thinking of, when my mother's key clicked in the lock? It was late, pitch dark outside, dark inside my memory too. She came into the living room and we were happy to see her, but not as much as we usually were, when her return did not mean your departure. We clung around your legs, wishing you both would stay.

I don't remember the interim.

What I remember: our sudden scrambling. Sharp, hurting voices. My brother leading me past your tangled, tripping feet, the door one of you was trying to slam on the other, my brother's stern voice: 'We should go now, Xanthi, we should go.'

'Some brother you've got there,' you said, years later, as though he was another gift you had given me.

Well, he needed to be. He was less than two years older but I never questioned his authority, his capacity to make a decision like that at the age of six or seven. When is it time to walk away? How hard should you try to stop them? When have you seen enough of your mum and dad shouting at each other for reasons you don't understand but know must be something to do with the way your dad disappears again after that for months and months and months?

You sent letters. We threw most of them away. Envelopes and words proving only that you weren't there. Now, years later, when I'm lying in the dark crying because you're dead, I think, You want to talk to him? Then why did you throw away all those fucking letters?

There is never enough. It is food and I need it to last.

One summer, all you sent me was an envelope full of postcards of the cave paintings at Pech Merle. The eight-thousand-year-old horses, the even more ancient red buffalo, the handprints, your handwriting on the back stating only the date, the place, the fact you'd been there. I remember opening the envelope, how it looked lying on the doormat, how impossible it was not to believe there'd be some real part of you inside. What I remember more sharply: the weight pressing through me when I saw that was all it was. Postcards, mostly blank. I flipped them each over, looking for clues, but there was nothing more. When you came back, all you talked about were those paintings. I tried to match your wonder. Tens of thousands of years those painted animals had waited in the dark to be found. I could imagine that. But I didn't know if I could wait that long.

I couldn't wait to read the poem you wrote for me, when I found out it existed. But you said I was too young. I saw my name on the contents page of your new book and you took it from me, hid it when you thought I couldn't see. But I snuck it from the shelf when you weren't looking, ran upstairs to lock myself in your bathroom. I was eight, high on my rebellion and the sound of you knocking, ordering me to give it back. I didn't waver. My eyes stayed glued for the duration of two pages. I read it twice before I opened the door. I never knew why you wanted to hide it. It's my favourite thing you ever made me. Forty-three lines. And the hundreds of times my eyes have traced the images, tracking word to word, trying to follow again how one thought gives way to another. It's called 'A Sealed Box for Xanthi'.

In many years from now, you'll read
These lines I write, when I am dead.
Why were you born, my darling, or
What is a person living for?

Let us assume these questions are
One question, all-the-more bizarre:
How should we approach this life,
Which murders us, the more we love?

In lines of love I have before
Written more,
Which I perceive small use to you, as you
Do what you do.
How may the music of my mind inspire
In you, who played with me for hours,
The living fire,
When all that's left of me is flowers?

Your life ago, the light of dawn
Shone in your eyes, five minutes born.
You had a look of fiery pride
In which my egotism died.

When you were one, or two, or three,
You had the measure of my heart;
And long before I could devise
A way for me
To instruct you in the art
Of being alive, you were heavenly-wise,
Drinking
Through a straw,
Conscious of compassion as a primary choice, a decision,
Which you enacted with precision,

And set me thinking.
And then I saw
Love precedes what we are living for.

Do you remember how we made a rocking-horse
Out of rubbish?
How you swung, in a swish, swish, swish,
An original emblem of the force
By which such love is known?
I rock you in the bone.
To have had such moments with you is bliss
Conscious of the kiss
With which we leave
This earth, on which we quarrel, love, and grieve.

Yes, I remember. The day you took us trawling the skips of Kentish Town, picking up scraps of wood and broken furniture that we took back to your flat and laid out in the garden, my brother and I set the task of measuring each piece while you sketched a plan on the back of an envelope. You were going to make us a rocking horse. You had tools, a workbench, nothing to do all day, a four-year-old and a six-year-old for your assistants.

It had to be the back of an envelope. 'Where all the finest plans are made,' you said.

You showed us the design, checking for our approval, measured our legs and arms to size it. You rolled up your sleeves and we got to work, handing you nails and hammers we already knew the names of, every now and then called over to feel the tug of the saw in our small, sticky hands. There was dowelling for the handles at the horse's brow, two curved slats for the rocking base, a coping saw to cut the shape of the head. It got dark and you made us fish fingers and chips and dropped us home, already planning the painting we'd do on our next visit. So for two weeks we held our breath, my brother and I, dreaming up colours and images for our new horse. I remember the sun that afternoon, the rocking horse standing proud and bare on a table you'd carried outside, the dirty old rags and turpentine and oil paints and old shirts for us to cover our clothes. The face, the eyes, the mane, the legs, the curved base, one side each for two children. You painted our names and took our instruction for the parts where our wishes outstripped our skill. The light died again, more fish fingers and chips, another trip home without our horse. We had to wait another week for the paint to dry. You knew our mum wouldn't want wet paint in her flat. Another week, and I knew you were coming.

We were playing on the living-room floor when you knocked. My mum opened the door and we saw the rocking horse in your arms, the colours of the paints deeper, having lost their shine. You set it on the floor and we fought over taking the first ride. I won, and the first thing I did was rock right over the horse's head to land on mine.

My brother didn't have time to take his turn. Our mum

insisted you take it back at once. 'She could've broken her neck!'

You scooped up the horse and carried it off without another word. A few weeks later, it reappeared, blunt tips fixed to its base, our mum's wary eyes tracking our rocking enough to suck the innocence but not the joy out of it.

Our mother to ourselves – is this another gift you gave us? No one to share her with, no one for her to share us with.

She told me once: 'I didn't think a man would leave his children. I didn't think he would be able to. It wasn't a part of my reality.' She never imagined she would be raising two children alone on benefits. I guess nobody does.

I remember her from this time like an ethereal underground spirit, backlit by the low light streaking through the basement windows, making us salt dough, chasing us with the vacuum cleaner, showing us her oil pastel drawings, portraits and still lifes that I thought she must have brought with her from some other life. When sewage came through the floor my brother and I splashed in it, delighted. She said the love between the three of us was worth more than anything we could buy, and I believed her. What does a three-year-old know about loneliness, about spending day after day without adult company, about unpaid bills and mounting debt?

Another time she told me: 'Those were the happiest

years of my life. I'd always wanted children. Now I had nothing to do but be with you.'

What does it mean to find gifts here, in the shock waves of your leaving?

It's like when you died and the world started rippling: time, feeling and physics no longer obeying their laws. I zoned out of conversations, found myself a decade earlier picking the seam of my schoolbag on your passenger seat, listening to Johnny Cash and talking about the *via negativa*. Or looked in the mirror and for the first time liked my own face, seeing yours in it. And do you know, when I walked past 'the graves of Abney Park' – which is a line from your poem – the day I was going to meet your wife and my sister to see about a place for the wake, and I was shaking, all grief-mad and zombie-eyed, I watched geometry give way to a void underground that sucked all the stones, trees, paths, benches, ivy into it.

When you were old and ill and then iller, it wasn't you giving us gifts any more. I came to see you, a tourist from the outside world, and brought you Kellogg's Cornflakes, salted cashew nuts, oil paints and paper and brushes, books you didn't read. I bought you condensed milk, too, your favourite kind, the type they only sell in Greece, and a can of Spam, because you liked to eat it sliced and fried. I took your watch to get a new strap and got the colour of the buckle wrong, though you never mentioned it. My brother brought you a laptop so you could watch films in bed. I brought you *Searching for*

Sugar Man and *Walk the Line* on DVD. He bought you a small, heavy bottle of single malt whisky and we brought our mother over to drink some. She brought you an apple crumble, and cream to eat it with and you ate it like a hungry child, laughing, and said it was just what your legs felt like – apple crumble – when you tried to walk down the stairs. The last thing I brought you was spanakopita, a home-made version of the Greek pastry you liked so much. I made you four and you ate one, saved the others to eat later.

But there was no later. You died, and all these things belonged to nobody again.

I didn't want the DVDs back, or the brushes, the mini spanakopitas still wrapped in foil, though your wife gave them to me anyway. My brother didn't want the whisky. He sold the laptop. Who knows what happened to the apple crumble? I didn't want the coelacanth fish I'd drawn you, either. The books I lent. I didn't want to see all your belongings abandoned, how they blushed, shamefaced, to have become so unnecessary. I wanted to see your hands on them. I wanted your teeth on them, your eyes. I wanted to hear your voice, asking for them.

And not only that, but I wanted to be the one you asked. I wanted to be there with you, safe inside a smile you invented the day I was born.

Because, that's it, isn't it? The only gift anybody really gives you – a version of the world, a version of yourself. A particular experience of life that is only possible between you. And when that person dies, the part of you that was created by them and was only present when you were with them – the thing that was between you – dies also. There is no one in the world and never will be again who will make you feel that way. Who will give my voice that particular timbre, my face that particular brightness, my blood that particular fizz.

If I think that I want you, it is always in the old sense of the word. Such a deep, cold lack.

You are what is wanted. You are what I lack.

I still have all the things you made for me, the letters I kept, your watch, your tools and turpentine and hog-hair brushes, your coelacanth. All these objects I pore over, arrange and rearrange, inspect and share and hide again, as though if only I could fit them together in the right order, turn them the right way, show them to the right person, some key would turn in the world and you would open the door and come back.

The philosopher

After your lung collapsed, you were sent for various scans and tests and a consultation was scheduled for the following Tuesday to give you the prognosis, leaving us for five nights in limbo. I spent the weekend fretting and googling 'lung cancer', talking to anybody who would listen about what my internet searches had thrown up. I watched the Wimbledon final, for once not bored by it, though I didn't know any of the rules or who was who. I could not sleep, and willed the time to disappear, exchanging Google for endless reels of baby animal videos when I started to feel like the anxiety would break me open.

Despite all this, I was not prepared for what Tuesday brought. I wasn't prepared for your voice on the end of the phone, asking so sincerely that I come to your house as soon as I could, that evening preferably, that I get hold of my brother, who was again not answering his phone, and bring him too. There was news you wanted to tell us together.

As well as waitressing, I worked as a self-employed tutor and Tuesday was my busiest day. I had lessons to teach. I went to them. I taught fractions and percentages and how to answer extended comprehension questions to get full marks in an exam and when I had finished I

XANTHI BARKER

took the bus to Highbury and Islington station where I had arranged to meet my brother. He was late. Ten minutes after the time we had arranged to meet he messaged me to say he'd be half an hour. I rang him to ask what had possibly kept him and he said he'd been fixing his shower. He told me not to be annoyed.

'What's the rush?' he said. 'He's not going anywhere. I have things to do. We've got to be civilised.'

Civilised. What was he talking about?

I listened, though. I always listened to my brother. And his certainty made me calmer. I had been standing outside the station chain-smoking and wondering why it was so hard to breathe. I bought a bottle of water and drank it and went into a pub to use the mirror and wash my face, fix my hair, put on mascara.

To be civilised.

I waited. Half an hour passed. I rang my brother again. He lived about a twenty-minute walk away, or a ten-minute bus ride, five minutes on the Tube. We had arranged to meet here so we could take the Tube to Seven Sisters and walk the fifteen minutes to your house from there. I rang you to let you know I was waiting for my brother, that we would be late. You were confused and I felt guilty and made excuses for my brother better than the excuses he had given me. I said he'd had work that had run over.

You told me to get there soon.

You didn't like lateness. You didn't like people not doing what they said they were going to do. My brother would

98

always point out the irony of this, that for so much of our childhood you would promise to see us and then cancel, or turn up weeks after we'd first arranged it, or disappear for months without saying anything, forget our birthdays – the usual absent father routine. Several times when we were small our mother refused to let you see us, or even plan to, because you let us down so many times that even the mention of you would leave us distraught.

Finally, almost an hour after we were supposed to meet, my brother arrived. I expected that we would get straight on the Tube, but he was hungry, he said. He had to get some food. He couldn't go if he didn't have food, he needed his strength.

'What? Why didn't you eat at home?'

'I didn't have any food at home. We'll get a taxi. I'll pay. We'll get there quicker anyway.'

He started walking towards the shop and I followed him, trying not to be annoyed. But inside the shop he spent ages choosing what to eat, and chose things that did not fit with my feelings about this evening, so that I asked if he didn't think it was a bit much, buying smoked salmon and artichokes when we were about to find out how long our dad had left to live.

'He's not dying right now,' he said. 'And what difference does it make anyway? I need to eat.'

Outside again, he rang a taxi and the company said it would be twenty-five minutes. I rolled a cigarette, scowling,

angry in that prickly sibling way where I wasn't ashamed
to say, 'I told you so.' But my brother was unmoved. So
we sat on the kerb on Upper Street while he ate his
smoked salmon and rocket with a fresh baguette and
artichokes, offering me bites while I worried that the taxi
would never arrive.

'Why does he have to be so grandiose about it,
summoning us to his house?' my brother said.

I said it sounded to me like it wasn't good news.

'Of course it's not good news. He's got cancer.'

My brother and I always disagreed about you. We'd
had different experiences of you, growing up. You had
been around, a regular live-in dad, for the first two years
of his life, while I was born (almost) into your absence.
He knew something of the loss of you. I never expected
anything else. He was angry with you in a way I didn't
know how to be. But also, I knew my brother. I knew this
coldness and reluctance was partly a way of mitigating
his fear. So although I was frustrated with him, after a
few minutes I stopped being annoyed and was relieved
to sit with him on the kerb waiting for the taxi while
he ate his fancy picnic dinner. It gave us time to talk,
time to think. After all, in many ways – and I think
you knew this – he'd been more of a dad to me than you
had been.

And when we finally arrived, you hugged both of us
so tightly that I was sure you had already forgiven us. I
apologised and my brother didn't and you said it didn't

matter, come and sit down. You were sitting propped up on your bed, the sun streaming through the skylight, a blanket pulled over your legs. You looked tanned and strong, surprisingly healthy in your clean clothes and combed hair – much more alive than last time I'd seen you. I sat cross-legged on the far side of the bed while my brother sat on the chair beside you. You did not wait. You did not make any preamble. You took our hands in each of yours and, without looking at either of us, told us what the doctor had told you.

It was lung cancer, stage 3. You had a tumour the size of a tennis ball in your left lung. It hadn't spread, but it was inoperable. Chemotherapy would be useless. There was no possibility of remission. The only treatment you'd be given would be palliative. In short, it was terminal.

You were going to die.

You were smiling as you told us. You explained it in the same way you always explained things – complicated ideas resolved into simple logical structures. You explained it as though it was something inevitable that could not therefore be regarded as negative, or contradicted. You said that, in fact, you had reached a point of repletion in your life and, though it might sound unbelievable, the diagnosis had come as a kind of relief.

We nodded. We met your eye when you turned to us. We said we understood.

In many ways, it was the denouement we might have imagined. You had always presented yourself as beyond pettiness, beyond greed, intensely rational and not-quite-human, a philosopher who paid little mind to what anyone else believed your values should be. Perhaps you told us or perhaps you implied that you wouldn't speak to the others like this, that you wouldn't say anything of this kind to your wife or to our sisters. What did it mean that you should find it easiest to announce your resignation from life to us, your youngest children? We were twenty-four and twenty-six. You would be missing so much of our lives.

I remember my brother speaking more than I did, and you – as you always did when it was the three of us – addressing him almost exclusively. My brother was transformed, his earlier resentment and ridicule replaced by sincerity, compassion and alarming articulacy. He was saying exactly what you needed someone to say, that's what I thought, while I became stupid and childish, saying things I didn't mean for the sake of saying something. I tried to join in the tone of stoical wondering, but I couldn't get it right, and sounded glib and strange. And yet all the time you continued to hold my hand and every now and then you turned to me and I could see a glisten in your eyes.

It struck me then that you were trying to persuade each other, each more afraid of this intimacy than the other, each more afraid of what could not be said. That perhaps, as the woman or as the youngest, wordlessly I had been given the task of holding the place of feeling, keeping it to one side so that you could look at each other and look away from it.

Death is easier if it is a relief. We were reassuring each other. None of us cried.

'Sitting there in the consultant's office, I understood what the doctor was saying from the outset. My wife and your sister were brilliant. I was lucky to have them there. They'd come prepared with a list of questions each but I knew from the first words the doctor spoke that none of it would be any use. I was a man staring into the face of his own mortality. That confrontation – it shakes you to the core. I could see it, just as the doctor was speaking. I wasn't listening to what she was saying. I was seeing it there. The very fact of my own mortality. It was only afterwards when your sister explained it all to me again on the drive home that I understood what had been discussed, in terms of treatment. They use the word treatment, though it will only be palliative.'

Palliative.

Had I met that word before? Now it buzzes with a sickening menace. Back then it can't have been more than a collection of syllables, an academic acquaintance. Palliative. Like taking painkillers for the flu. It won't cure you but it'll make you feel better. Something of the sound of 'palate' to it, 'palatable', olfactory and gourmet, or prehistoric like 'palaeolithic'. To make something more palatable, to make it historic and therefore acceptable, to ease you out of life and into history in a neat, aesthetic way. Etymology by homophone, you wouldn't approve of that, would you? It's the kind of purposeful mistake I would perform to make you laugh.

'Xanthi!' you would say in mock outrage. 'If you look over here in this dictionary I've got, I can show you palliative is from the Latin verb "palliare" meaning: to cloak.'

To cloak. Well, exactly – a cloak thrown over the horror of it. You were sitting there with my brother weaving another one. I didn't want a cloak. I wanted to know.

'What's the *palliative* treatment then?' I said. 'What are they going to do?'

My brother stopped mid-sentence. He had been saying something almost incomprehensible about the 'abyssal void beyond existence'.

You turned, frowning, to look at me. Then you smiled your wounded smile. The one you saved for the questions I was not supposed to ask. There were several seconds during which I could see you deciding how to answer. Then you patted my hand, letting go of it, and leaned back against the headboard.

'There'll be an operation, first of all,' you explained. 'They'll put a stent in to reopen my lung.' You turned to us one at a time, no longer a philosopher but a teacher once more. 'Do you know what a stent is?'

My brother shook his head and I stopped nodding.

You put your two first fingers up and pressed the tips together, miming pulling them apart with some difficulty.

'It's like a Chinese finger trap. It's a tube made of wire mesh that can be pulled narrow and long and then opened up into a relatively strong tube. It's a remarkably simple device. They'll cut through the tumour to make an airway and then push the stent through, hoping that when it's in it'll be strong enough to hold. This technology is nothing new, in fact it's quite ancient. Like so much of medicine – my new hip, for example – the principles are basic Newtonian physics. It's just mechanics.'

You smiled, your eyebrows rising way up, and upturned your palms, as though in proof of the simplicity. I asked when you would have the operation and you said as soon as possible, in the next few weeks.

'Once I have my lung back, I should be as good as I was before. The only difference at the moment, you see, is that I'm operating on one lung. I'm not really sick, I just don't have the wind power to move around, which is very annoying.'

'Exactly,' my brother said. 'You've been living with this thing for years, probably. It can't have got to that size out of nowhere.'

You tipped your head. 'Well spotted. Yes. That's just what the doctor said. By the size of it, they think it could have been decades.'

Decades, I thought. Are you serious?

'Decades,' my brother said, nodding. 'So what do they think could have caused it?'

Decades?

'One thought was that it might have stretched all the way back to the late sixties when I was stripping all that furniture. There were no safety precautions back then. I used to work in a pair of shorts and a T-shirt, no mask or gloves. I had a giant tank of caustic soda and I dipped the furniture in, leaning over it. I would have been inhaling it on a daily basis. It may very well have started then.'

Before I was born. Before my brother was born.

My dad has had cancer my whole life.

'That's crazy, isn't it?' my brother said. 'That's more than forty years. And you never knew.'

As though it was some miracle.

I felt dizzy. I tried to mimic my brother's expression. I tried to mimic your expression. I tried not to think about the tennis ball-sized knot of mutinous cells in your chest, tightening their grip around your lung. All that time. Days as a child I had sat on your knee resting my cheek on that exact place, playing with the silver chain at your neck, inches from the thing that would kill you. If we could know the chaos inside a person. If we'd had X-ray vision. If we could have guessed what that shadow was, hovering over your heart.

It was late by the time we left. The sun had gone down. We hugged you. When I got to the door of your room, I went back to hug you again. I told you I loved you and felt immediately embarrassed, self-serving. It wasn't something we said to each other often, if at all, and the words spoken now sounded wrong, as though borrowed. Whether I loved you or not wasn't the point. What did it matter if I loved you now?

Outside, my brother rubbed his hands over his face and sighed. He would not say anything until we had walked to the end of the street. Without looking at me, he called us a taxi. The company said it would be half an hour, so he said it didn't matter, we'd find one on the high street. We walked and I watched the side of his face. He was my big brother, I was counting on him to know how to react, to give shape to my own feelings. But he just kept pawing at his face and talking about the taxi. He was supposed to meet someone at eight, he said. We were going in opposite directions, so I said I would take the bus, and we hugged goodbye outside a minicab office.

He squeezed me against him until my ribs hurt and all the breath was gone from my lungs. 'It's going to be all right,' he said. 'He's ready for it. He's been preparing for this his whole life.'

SSB's Dictionary

Dipsomaniac: a person who undergoes extreme personality change after drinking alcohol. May or may not be an alcoholic. Often applied to negative changes but applies to positive changes too.

Sixteen white stallions

The house you built with my mother in Greece was mythical to me during my early childhood. I knew the stories, the smells, the place names, the names of our friends there. I thought of them as 'our' friends, the house as 'our' house, though I had never been anywhere further than the Isle of Wight. At least not that I could remember. In fact, I had been to Greece once, as a baby. The story of this trip was an assemblage of contradictory facts: the four of us went together, though you and my mother had already split up, but there are photos of you laughing with her, kissing each other. My mother tells how I learned to walk in the sand and you built us a yellow boat and sailed us in it across the mouth of the river we have been swimming in for decades since. There are several photos of you in your jean shorts wading in the green water, my brother in red swimming trunks and me in a white bonnet and nappy, my limbs tan and fat with milk.

It was ten years before my brother and I would return with you. During this time we went twice with our mother, and though later I learned how painful these trips were for her, to us they felt like weeks in paradise. We spent the days on the beach playing imaginary games or building giant networks of sandcastles and moats. The evenings we spent sitting on terraces eating sugary cakes while our mother gossiped with the women of the village, or drinking Fanta from curved, icy bottles in the cafe and cracking monkey nuts while our mother smoked and laughed with the old men. After, we stayed up late playing card games on the balcony, marvelling at the black sky and expanse of stars and how our mother came back to life, grew young and cheerful again among the wild herbs and crickets and sunlight. Since retraining in a new career and going back to work, on top of having sole responsibility for two children, she was exhausted. But on holiday she was twenty-seven again, myriad futures still glittering in front of her.

So we knew parents were liable to change character on holiday. But we could not have anticipated how different you would be. Our trips to Greece with you were nothing like the trips with our mother. It was a different house, a different country, though it had the same smells, same stones, same stories. And you were a different person – though it was true we had little to go on, since we had never spent more than a day with you, picked up after breakfast and dropped back in time for bed. You did not know us in pyjamas, holding toothbrushes, needing baths or waking up afraid in the night, and we did not know you after dark. You were a man made of daylight, oil paints, fish fingers and chips and purposeful car rides.

At first, you had suggested you would take only my brother. He came home one evening from seeing you and announced, full of pride, that you were going to take him to Greece that half-term and show him how to build a trellis. I was devastated. You'd never mentioned anything like this to me. I cried myself to sleep for weeks while my mother explained to me that it was important for my brother, that you wanted to have this special thing with him. It was because he was a boy. Fathers and sons did special things. I had never wanted to be a girl, but at that moment felt my femininity as an outrage.

It wasn't only that. We'd just moved in with my mum's boyfriend and I'd started a new school, changes I was finding it hard to adjust to. It seemed obvious to me that nobody in the world wanted to be around me. But when my brother admitted he didn't want to go alone anyway, my mum called you and told you how upset I was.

You had no idea, you said, that I would be interested. Of course I could come.

I almost didn't believe it, that you would change your plans so easily. But it was agreed, you told me the next time I saw you. All three of us would go together. Girl or not, I too would learn how hands cared for houses, how they could turn lime and water into cement, clean the rust off railings, tease the accidental vine from the rubble below the balcony and thread it up through wire and those sun-glinting railings to make a trellis where every summer grapes would grow.

We first went in the spring of 1999, when I was ten

and my brother twelve. The trip was a success – you genuinely enjoyed the time with us, we did not alienate you with our childish needs, and most importantly for our mother, nobody died, incurred serious injury or lost any expensive or irreplaceable possessions. You took us again the following May, and after that we started going in October too. For four years, these half-term trips were regularities in our lives, and we grew easier with you, though we were growing up and our bodies and lives were changing. If on the first trip I was a child whose elder brother put her to bed and woke up in the night to shush her bad dreams, by the last I was a teenager who swore and smoked weed with you and spent hours lying downstairs, alone, reading the novels full of sex and violence and anger that adult guests – friends, relatives, lovers, I didn't know – had left there.

But for all those years, the format of the trips remained the same. In the days there would be a history tour, your monologue running us through tombs and amphitheatres, ruined castles and sacrificial sites, while my brother and I competed to ask the best questions, make the most insightful comment. In the afternoons we'd go to the beach where you'd make a desk of bamboo and stones and work for several hours while I swam and my brother tried to drown me or get me to help build a dam to change the course of the river. When you'd finished whatever you were working on, you'd come and join us, if what we were doing was interesting enough. You liked to oversee the dam-building, complimenting my brother's engineering while I tried and failed to impress you with cartwheels. We competed to be your best student, your biggest fan, remembering what you'd said and picking it apart with the logic we'd learned from you. We read the books you told us about, used your language to analyse it. If my brother seemed to be winning your favour at any time, I would tease both of you, twisting the same language into nonsense until you were relieved when I asked a serious question to prove I understood.

As we got older, our attitudes shifted. I became more vehement in my devotion – every move and remark I made anticipated your interest and approval. My brother stopped trying so hard, or tried to engage you only on topics he could also talk about, like the new *Lord of the Rings* film or world politics. In private he complained he found you overbearing, exhausting, but it made no difference to my certainty you preferred him to me.

After the beach we'd go straight home, unless you'd run out of wine. Then we'd stop off at the winery where men with handlebar moustaches and cigarettes hanging from their mouths took us inside the dark corrugated-iron shed and laughed at our small shoulders drooping under the weight of gallon bottles. Back home, my brother would chop firewood with an axe you taught him to sharpen until he was sweating and red-cheeked, his hair in tufts. I'd peel potatoes, cutting them into the letters of our names like our mum always did, ready to deep-fry for chips, the deep-fat fryer being our main kitchen equipment. Chips and souvlaki, that's what we ate every night, except I was vegetarian so ate only chips. You were childishly afraid of both cucumbers and tomatoes, and without encouragement, my brother and I were happy to forgo vegetables altogether.

One night, you attempted to make some kind of risotto. Our mother had suggested we ate something healthy, you said. But when you served it, it was grey, gravelly and rancid-smelling. None of us could manage a mouthful. You laughed, baffled by your misadventure, and we threw it away and ate Marmite on toast instead. This was your favourite meal, the only thing you would eat if left to your own devices – cold, burnt toast with scrapes of fridge-solid butter, Marmite smeared thick so it stung your nose. You had a knack, which I've tried to learn, for relishing the things other people would throw away. But not the risotto – that's how bad it was. After that we settled back to souvlaki and chips. We'd get home in the early evening and you'd set us to work cutting chips and preparing the barbecue, while you got to work on the wine.

The bottles were the kind with handles attached to the lids, labels stuck on the side, handwritten with pictures of grapes. You only bought red wine, but in the clear plastic bottles it was pinkish, translucent. You would decant it into a copper jug and then pour small measures from that into a tumbler, sitting at the red metal three-legged table drinking glass after glass, not speaking, listening to whatever music we'd put on. By the time we sat down to eat, you were glassy-eyed. My brother and I would lay the table and we'd each cover everything in salt and you would start talking again and not stop. You knew how to tell stories, weaving them into each other like our own personal Arabian Nights. But what were your stories saving us from? What menaces did you see there, swirling beyond our small heads?

'Do you know what you've just reminded me of?' you might start, though neither of us would know what it was we'd done or said to remind you.

Regardless, we'd nod, insisting yes, we were listening.

The story would continue, you pointing, frowning, drawing each of us in at different moments. 'Yes, I remember, it was just down there by that rock. If you look over the railings just behind you, Xanthi, you'll see. I was setting out for a walk one afternoon. I'd been digging two centuries of animal shit out of the downstairs room, trying to make a bathroom at your mother's insistence. I was out here on my own, one spring. Your mother was back in London with you, Daniel. I needed to get out of the house. It had got much too hot to work, so I made myself a picnic and took it down into the valley to have lunch. But just down there, around the track, right before the great wheel for grinding grain that this village is named after, which I've taken you both to see, if you remember. Right there, a young hound spotted me, a mongrel. He took a liking to me and followed me all the way. We walked right across the mountain, up into the orange garden that I've taken you both to before, if you remember. I found a place under a tree on a rock in the shade and he sat down next to me. He was very friendly. Of course I had to share my picnic with him. I was delighted that he wanted to join me. We had a short snooze afterwards – a siesta – and walked back together to the village. I went up to the house and he went down the track and I never saw him again. It was wonderful. You know, that is a special kind of friendship.'

My brother and I would offer some kind of comment, responses designed to show we had understood your message rather than to add our own. Then something would trip into something else, and soon another story would begin. You'd set the scene, some sharp, tantalising insight into your state of mind at the time, other people summed up in heroic, snap anecdotes or words you used as though they were common parlance – the Turncoat, the Flibbertigibbet, the Ditherer, the Good and the Great. Everything had such drama to it – a poised kind of awe, not quite exaggeration, emotions pushed to their limit. I hear you still when I tell stories, use adjectives for feeling rather than truth-value.

You'd tell us about the women you'd loved, your friends, our family members, as though you were revealing to us great legends, as significant as any other mythical creatures we might have heard about. Our mother especially featured in these stories, bound as she was to the house. You told us about the months you'd spent here together, the summer she first came out here; stories of the villagers. How the village president, a barber, had the sweetest singing voice and would sing old folk ballads in an improbable tenor while he clipped your hair with his eyes half shut. How the policemen who came to see the tiler one summer were whisked off in the back of the engineer's Toyota to buy six gallons of *tsipouro* – the illegal overproof spirit made from grape skins – from a secret location up the mountain instead. How the engineer spent night after night when he returned from the navy up those same mountains, hiding out in the back of his Toyota, drinking *tsipouro* and shooting cats. How nobody knew what changed him, but it was something to do with his kindness now, his generosity, that light in his eye.

You told these stories without listening for our reactions, smoking and drinking until it was pitch dark and even the staccato voices from the cafe had died down. The only time you would acknowledge us was to set us tasks, which mostly I took up. Fill your jug, fetch your cigarettes, go inside and put on exactly the right music. That was my favourite task, and the most terrifying. You pronounced it 'moo-si-key', an approximation of the Greek, saying, 'Xanthi! We need moo-si-key. You must go inside and choose exactly the right music for this moment. It's got to be the *right* one. Make no mistake.' I'd go inside, heart pounding, looking through the hundreds of sticky, faded cassette tapes – Bob Dylan, Van Morrison, Jimi Hendrix, The Doors – certain I'd get it wrong. But I never got it wrong. That was part of your charm, part of the way you made us feel loved. Always, although we were convinced it wouldn't be, what we could offer you was exactly what you wanted.

I loved to choose the songs, to learn your music. I loved to hear your glee at songs you hadn't heard in years. The *duende*, that's what you said you were looking for – the moment of transcendence, the part of a song that breaks a person. I learned later that it's a word flamenco musicians use as the highest compliment. You never told us that. Just used the word like you used all your idioms, as though their meaning was obvious, at least in the world you inhabited – and wasn't that where we most wanted to be?

Bruce Springsteen's *Born in the U.S.A.* was one of your favourites, in particular 'No Surrender'. Every time that song came on you would stop in the middle of whatever you were telling us and say, 'Listen. Wait. Listen to this.'

We listened all the way through while you whispered your favourite lines, tears springing to your eyes.

'That's it. That's it – it's not what you're taught in school, listen – a three-minute record, Xanthi – that's where the real learning is.' At the end of the song, every time, you made me promise to play it at your funeral. You wanted it played as the coffin was carried in.

'Of course, Daddy, you asked already. Yes, I promise you.'

So many of my values and ideals, so much of my self was formed on that balcony to the ravings of my drunk dad and a soundtrack of sixties, seventies and eighties pop music. It wasn't just music we were playing, not just stories you were telling, but an intricate structure of meanings you were building, your heroes and principles and borrowed words echoing off each other so that all we could do was try to hold on to as much as possible, record the marvel of you in our still-forming minds, as you connected firewood, shooting cats, Bruce Springsteen to history, life, death, the consciousness of a table, a fly, the cicadas, the monotone beep of the submarine owl, the street lights that robbed the stars from the night, that hadn't been there a few years before.

I wanted to stay in those hours forever, filling your copper jug and playing just the right music and hearing about all that past that had somehow begun me. I wanted never to go home again, to let my school uniform rot at the bottom of the laundry basket while I drank in the smoky dark wrapped in your moth-eaten jumper, saved my maths brain for building calculations, befriended stray dogs instead of unfathomable schoolgirls. I wanted to pass you your Rothmans and laugh, unheard, with my brother, knowing the ends of the stories before you'd told them, as you'd told them so many times before, forever.

But the night would keep passing. The fire would die out. My brother would bring it back to life with the bellows the way you'd shown him. The ash would fly up and land on our hair and eyelashes, the jumpers it had got cold enough to put on. The crickets would get louder and your voice would get softer and the words would lose their edges and you'd stop looking at us to check we were listening at all. I'd feel your attention slipping away from me and I'd go over to climb up on to your knee. You'd wrap an arm around me like a seat belt, without any discernible affection, though every now and then when you were making a point you'd squeeze me, or shake me like a rag doll for emphasis. You reeked of meat and cigarettes and wine and I thought how this must be what it meant to love someone: to bear the revulsion of being so close up. The village would be silent, all the other lights out. Perhaps I or my brother would decide to turn the music off. My brother would stop rebuilding the fire. Then it would be just the dogs howling, the trill of crickets and the occasional roar of a single car coming up the mountain.

And you, Daddy, still going on.

You'd start to pass out, wake up, pass out. You'd lose a story halfway through and start on another, or start again. Your stories would be interspersed with lines from your poetry, as though the poems had always belonged to the stories that way, as though that was where you'd first found them. Soon you stopped referring to us at all, or stopped talking altogether. You'd push me off your knee and go inside to fill your copper jug yourself, or stumble downstairs to the toilet, putting the music back on when you returned. At a certain point you'd get up and walk around to the other side of the house where the sky was clearer. You would sit there late into the night. Once or twice you took us around to sit with you, but mostly you were no longer conscious of us when my brother stood up and said, 'Come on, Xanthi, let's go inside.'

My brother would pour water on the fire to put it out and then we'd go inside and shut the door. We'd brush our teeth, put pyjamas on, get into bed. The house is about ten metres by three, all one room, with another bed downstairs in the bathroom that you slept in. My brother and I slept upstairs, him in the big bed and me in a camp bed opposite the door. He would come and sit on the edge of my bed like our mother would have done, making sure I was warm and safe. He'd tell me he loved me – something he'd never say at home – and hug me, tell me not to worry, no one could get in.

But I wasn't worried. I was never afraid. I didn't realise until later that my brother was – that all the parenting he gave me he needed for himself, that what those trips meant to him was a week of acting the role of my father, my protector. He'd turn out the light, check the axe was inside, lock and barricade the door. There was another door downstairs where you could come in, though this wasn't something we ever discussed with you. Perhaps my brother felt if you were too drunk to work that out you deserved to sleep outside.

In the dark, while I started to sink into sleep, my brother would be more lively than he'd been all night, and because I was almost as enthralled by him as I was by you, we'd stay up for hours talking about our friends, computer games, music, the philosophical problems you'd got us thinking about.

How does something come from nothing?

Who made better music, Interpol or The Doors?

Could *Donkey Kong Country* really be completed in under an hour?

What does it mean not to exist?

Was my brother talking to cover his anxiety, trying to work back to some approximation of safety? I was just happy to have you both to myself.

Then one October we flew out alone to Greece – you had been there several weeks already – to find you had made new friends and invited them into our idyll.

'We're going to have guests!' you announced on the drive back from the airport. 'A taxi driver poet. A brilliant man, sensitive to the world in an extremely unusual way. I met him quite by accident in a cafe in Olympia. I've invited him for dinner with us on Thursday with his wife.'

I was thrilled. To be introduced to your friends, for them to visit the house as though it was ours, as though we were the kind of family who had visitors, had friends – the idea delighted me. It was Sunday when we arrived and the prospect of the dinner hung there all week as proof of our togetherness, a special event in a week that was all special to me. My brother asked how you had met him and you explained that you got talking to him when you noticed he had a book by Odysseus Elytis on his table.

'Now Odysseus Elytis, children, do you know who that is?'

Of course we did. Thirteen and fifteen years old, but we knew the name of the poet who had first brought you to Greece, how his spirituality, his version of surrealism, was what distinguished him from all British poets of that time.

'Well, a taxi driver with a great love of Odysseus Elytis – he is of profound interest to me.'

Every night that week leading up to the dinner your stories were punctuated with memories of this meeting. We, or at least I, was convinced that on Thursday we would witness two poets in action, would listen in on the kind of serious conversation that I had only dreamed of or read about. The day came and we went to see some tombs, went to the beach, went to pick up some wine, the usual routines, and then came home to get ready. The sun was already going down and the barbecue lit when it occurred to you that our guests might want more than souvlaki and chips. You panicked. I'd never seen you flustered before.

Greeks are famous for their hospitality, their banquets, you said, we'd have to improvise. 'Xanthi! Can't you fix something up?'

I knelt in front of the cupboard, rooting through the dusty, cobwebbed shelves. Marmite, spaghetti, canned sardines, condensed milk. A jar of pickles, a can of peppers. I took a few things out. But before I could get started, there was a shout from up on the track and you clapped your hands and went out, reappearing a few minutes later with our guests.

The taxi driver was squarish, solid-looking, with a fountain of ragged grey-black curls and leathery, tan skin. His wife had neat hair, a neat dress, a small handbag and smart shoes. And then there was their daughter. None of us had anticipated there would be a daughter. She had hair like her dad, but tamer, held back tightly with an Alice band, and wore glasses, a long, floral dress and sturdy sandals. She was taller than me, in fact more of a woman than me in every way, though as you kept reminding me she was almost a year younger, turning thirteen next month. She was also the only one of us who spoke both English and Greek, and therefore by default the facilitator of all conversation. She set to work helping me in the kitchen – mixing a salad of canned vegetables, emptying olives from jars, cutting up feta – and though I had to show her where things were kept, it wasn't long before I was her sous-chef. I grew anxious at her expertise, her orders and my mistakes. She kept stepping outside to translate something for you, or to answer a question of yours that I'd been certain was meant for me, before coming back in to show me a better method of peeling potatoes, or tossing compliments to my brother on the hard work he put into chopping wood.

It became clear quite early on that the taxi driver didn't know as much about poetry as you'd imagined. Nor was he too interested in talking about Odysseus Elytis, beyond what the two of you had discussed the other day. You discussed the building of the house, the traditional style of the roof and the exposed rafters. The taxi driver scolded you for letting the cacti swallow the garden. The mother asked about a painting that was hanging on the wall but did not reply once you had explained the connection between it and a poem you'd written in 1965. My brother and I tried to help, as did the daughter, but every time you turned to me and I thought you would respond, instead you told me again how brilliant she was.

'This young woman!' you kept saying. 'Twelve years old, younger than you, Xanthi, and she can switch between two languages like an angel from heaven.'

By the time we sat down to eat, I couldn't stand to look at her.

You sat in your usual chair at the end of the table, the daughter beside you, her parents on her other side. My brother took the last solid chair and the last side of the table, and I was left with the broken stool at the corner, though happily I was next to you. My brother served the meat.

Everybody ate, with more or less enjoyment. The taxi driver complimented my brother's souvlaki. The mother ate one with bread and canned peppers. My brother and you ate how you always did – as though ravenous and eating the finest food in the world. I picked at my chips, eating more of my fingers than my food. The daughter, watching me, asked several times why I didn't take something else as well.

As usual, and no more slowly, you got drunk. The taxi driver couldn't drink because he was driving. His wife was nursing her first glass, of which the daughter tried a few sips. As usual, you began telling your stories. As usual, you were not really interested in any response. But tonight my brother and I were not listening. My brother kept looking at me. I kept my eye on the daughter, stealing occasional glances at the taxi driver, wondering why he wasn't who you'd said he was. The night went on and on. I remember you turning to hand me your copper jug to be filled, my satisfaction at knowing what you needed. I brought it back full and you filled another glass, offering it again to our guests who once again refused. Soon after that any dialogue there had been died out completely. And still your stories went on. But tonight, every now and then, like an echo, they were interspersed with the daughter's translations.

It got dark. The crickets got louder. You were really slurring; your eyes as though they were looking straight through the world, straight back inside your own head. You were running out of topics, perhaps aware you were losing your audience, when you came to the subject of the daughter. You spoke about her intelligence, her sensitivity. The rarity of her kind of mind. She translated this, too, and her parents nodded.

I wished you'd stop. I wished they'd leave. I wished my brother would stand up and tell me it was time to go to bed. I fought the urge to stand up anyway, to go inside and lock the door. But nobody moved. You continued your speech. She continued translating. She was laughing now, looking at the table, perhaps embarrassed by the immodesty of translating your praise. I didn't understand what she'd done to invoke this in you – she seemed so unspecial to me. I hated her, then, and hated you. And more than that, I hated the nothing-girl that the two of you had made me.

Then you said something that I would never forget, that still cuts me to remember. You took a breath, looking around at all of us, up at the stars, down at your arms folded across your chest.

'I would give sixteen white stallions for your daughter.'
That's what you said.
'Sixteen white stallions.'
You said it again.
The whole mountain held its breath except you.
Then the daughter translated it.
You said it several times, nodding and repeating it, as though pleased with yourself and with the image. As though it was a good thing, exactly the right thing to say to these people, her parents. I guess you must have thought

it was – a poet's compliment, slightly outrageous, for a child full of potential, something you might have said or heard yourself, decades ago, in the Colony Room. But any other meaning slipped away as the parents stiffened and frowned. Not noticing, you repeated the phrase again.

The daughter did not translate it this time.

The parents looked at each other. They shifted in their seats. My brother and I looked at each other. We shifted in our seats. Even I, in the prickly heat of my jealousy, knew my dad had said something terrible.

Sixteen white stallions.

I pictured them, all these huge white horses, and wished I couldn't. I didn't know what I was looking at. What I was too young or ignorant to know, whether the feeling I had was worse than what it was or not nearly bad enough. I couldn't look anybody in the eye but it didn't matter – nobody else could either. The daughter had lost her glow. Her mother lost the final dregs of her smile. The taxi driver lost the softness in his voice.

I remember you snorting, lighting a cigarette into the silence. I remember that soon after that, they left. We listened to them get into their car and drive away, heard the roar of the engine as it travelled back down the mountain. Then my brother and I took the things inside and left you to your wine. It wasn't fully dark yet. The shouts from the cafe were still dying down. We said goodnight and your face lifted for a moment, a vague smile dismissing us. Inside, we brushed our teeth, put our pyjamas on. Then my brother came and sat on the edge of my bed.

'He's crazy,' he said.

'That girl was weird.'

'She was just a normal girl. She was just some normal, boring girl.'

'She *was* boring.'

'I felt sorry for her. You should feel sorry for her. He's mad. What was he talking about? They thought he was a maniac.'

'They didn't say anything.'

My brother bit his nails, picked at the cuff of his pyjama sleeve. 'Forget about it, Xanthi. We're going home in two days.' Then, surprising me with his certainty about the meaning of what had happened, he added, 'She wasn't even pretty at all.'

We didn't understand anything. We had no tools to do so. We didn't know which parts of you came from the world of poets, which from the regular world of adults, which were only madness. To me it was further proof of your obsession with intelligence, that I could never provide enough of. Yet we knew that whatever we thought of you, these people had thought something else. That was enough to knock from under us the fragile ground we shared with you. I remember feeling bad, really bad, like it was our fault somehow that they'd left, that there was none of the literary talk you had imagined, like it was my fault in particular that you had hurt their daughter. Perhaps if I'd learned Greek. Or been kinder to the daughter.

But more than that, I wanted to know what it was in her that had brought out that prideful possessiveness. Sixteen white stallions you would have given for her, and you never even wanted me to be born.

On the last day, Saturday, you took us to Olympia. You liked to sit at the tables under the prehistoric oak tree there, you said, no other reason. We went to have a drink in that cafe on the main square and soon we noticed the taxi driver sitting a few tables over. You waved, called out hello. The taxi driver ignored us. We finished our drinks, paid and left. It was a long drive, we had to get home to pack.

'He was busy,' you said. 'Working. People are like that sometimes.'

My brother and I looked at each other. Was that the moment that broke something in our respect for you, that put a false note in all your glory-days stories, after?

You really had no idea.

I couldn't love you for months after that. That was the first trip I came back from crying, vowing never to talk to you again, beginning a cycle that would go on for years – right up until you died, in fact. Over a decade and a half later it seems almost farcical to me – our dinner from dusty cans, your early optimism, your almost medieval imagery – and yet no less painful for everyone involved.

It's a story I tell now for comic effect, though as a

teenager I'd tell it to shock people, to explain why, yes, I really did hate my dad. I could exploit the story, because I knew how it sounded, and I wanted to hurt you, to take revenge in my own small way. But I can see now that the shame of it, the feeling of worthlessness I was trying to put into you had been eating into me this whole time. I'd taken the parents' scorn as scorn for us also, horror at our seedy family. I'd soaked up all the confused feelings of rejection and disgust as though they were directed at me. I didn't realise that you were a man, totally independent of me, who could do bad things that had nothing to do with me. I didn't realise that you could do things that had no sense or purpose. But the taxi driver and his wife, even the daughter, what did they make of us – my brother and me? These two silent children in the dark, open mountains waiting on the whims of their slurring, impervious dad.

We were used to it, by then. We knew what to do. Perhaps that was what hurt the most about their reaction: the fact that they didn't. They couldn't cope with you, and that made it all the more obvious how difficult it was for us to do so.

The next morning you were up first, as usual, washing-up done, clean shirt on, greeting us with the lovely smell of burnt toast. You opened what you called 'Cafe Esmeralda' at the red metal table and took our toast orders by precise width – two centimetres for my brother, eight millimetres for me. You poured us tea and orange juice and teased us, playing along with our games and jokes. We talked about our dreams and I bossed you around, pretending to be strict, or fetched things for you, swung on the swing while you tidied up. Really, I think now, that's what I went for, kept going back for – the mornings with the village noises and Arleta, the Greek folk singer you liked to play, and the way the light came through the window and how clean, bright and new you were, my magic dad returned to make the early hours golden.

We never mentioned that night again. Would you have remembered, if I'd told you?

Sixteen white stallions and however many years that feeling has stayed in me, a hot, deep shame, a permanent inexplicable badness.

One friend says to me, 'It's like you're embarrassed to be yourself,' and I laugh so much with recognition that I almost cry, thinking, Yes exactly.

So much of this I find absurd, and uncomfortable, and yet it is all inside me – the chauvinist intellectual, the oblivious baby boomer, the mystic holding the keys to a secret world of meaning, the man who went to Greece to build a house to write a poem in – all these fragments of you, like shards of a mirror reflecting versions of myself I don't recognise, don't know how to integrate.

Would you have remembered – or are there things it is always better to forget?

The poet

T here were two main elements to your treatment. Repeatedly we were assured that neither would be any more than palliative, though in the end I wasn't convinced they were even that. The first was the operation to put in the stent so you could breathe again. This happened in August in a specialist lung hospital in Chelsea. I remember going to see you, walking down the sunlit tree-lined boulevards of Kings Road, the stucco-fronted houses, the luxury of it all, like the marble floor in the hospital, so different from other hospitals I'd been in. I found your ward and you were sitting up in bed, which surprised me, braced as I was for wounds, drips, drowsiness, blood.

You were sitting up in bed, beaming.

'Daddy?' I said.

You waved me over and threw your arms around me in a great bear hug, shaking me and patting my shoulder.

'Do you know what's happened today?' you said.

'They fixed your lung? It worked? You can breathe better?'

You shook your head. 'Oh, that's nothing. No.'

I stared at you. *Have they fixed your lung or not? Are you all right? Did something go wrong? What happened?*

'What, then?' I managed to say.

'I'll tell you what – the proofs for *The Land of Gold* arrived this morning.'

You had received a text from your publisher just after you regained consciousness to say they should have arrived in the post this morning and you sent your wife home to collect them. I wondered how she must have felt, leaving you delirious after a general anaesthetic, telling all the doctors about your work and what she was crossing London to bring back for you.

It was then I understood what was in the ripped brown envelope on your lap. Nothing medical at all, but an unbound manuscript, an inch of paper – the proofs of your new book. You removed it, evened the papers by tapping them on your lap, and turned them round so I could see the front plate. You laid it carefully on your legs, turning the pages one at a time so I could admire the typeface, the layout, the red and green lines and words where you had begun your corrections already. You turned to a section I knew well – 'Ten Zonulets'.

'Look here,' you said. 'See? They've moved this word down to the next line, but it needs to be up here with the rest. It's the way the poem looks to the eye which is so important when you have very few words like this.'

I nodded, taking in the word, the page, your shaking hand, your hospital gown, your silvery stubble, your serious eyes, serious voice, and the beeps behind you, the plastic tag measuring your pulse attached to your finger. Then I realised you were more in the page than you were beside me, because you frowned and started to pat around the bed, locating your pen and drawing another red line under a word.

Then your face relaxed and you looked up at me, bright again. 'This, Xanthi,' you said, shaking the document, 'is the best part of the entire process. The proofs. The proof of all the work you've done. A real object in the world. I have to look through and mark it up like this, cover it in all this red and green pen, yes, but that's nothing really – what matters is that it exists.'

I have a photo of you from that afternoon, your shoulders still broad under your hospital gown, your glasses on and grey hair combed back, your grin broad above the paper proofs gripped in your hands.

Your wife came back and stood beside your bed waiting for us to finish, her expression solemn and still. She had been to see the doctor to learn how the operation had gone, because you could not remember anything that had been said. She explained the outcome to us, and I watched you strain to understand, or perhaps it was only a strain to listen, when what you wanted to concentrate on was in your hands. The operation had been successful, the lung had been reinflated, they had cut into the tumour and the stent had gone in; if you didn't notice an improvement in your breathlessness immediately it would be because your lung was still inflamed. The fix wasn't permanent. The stent had a lifespan. Sooner or later the tumour would crush it again.

You nodded, your teeth gritted, the effort on your face palpable. She began to list the medicines you would need to take, the new ones and new doses of old ones, the schedule of tests before you could go home.

All three of us knew you weren't listening, and when she had finished, almost in apology, you turned to me and said, 'You see how complicated it all is?'

I nodded.

Your wife said you needed something to eat, and that she'd check what time they would bring the dinner around, what it would be.

You were irritated then. 'I'm fine, thank you, for the moment. I'm completely fine. And in fact I have a lot of work to do.' You frowned and held up your proofs – proof now of so many things it was impossible to give voice to.

Your wife looked hurt, I noticed, noticing you also refusing to notice. I caught her eye and we stood up. 'Shall we leave you to it then?' I said.

Certain then that you would be left alone, you relaxed, and kissed your wife and gave me another shaking, patting bear hug goodbye. Your wife and I walked downstairs together. She told me again what would happen now, what the stent could and couldn't do, what the other treatments were. I listened, recording facts and dates and possibilities. I asked her how she was, what she was doing that evening, if she had somewhere to be. She asked me the same questions, and I thought how strange it was to be doing this huge thing together and yet have so little knowledge of each other's lives.

So I did not know what to do, where to look, what to say when, as we were saying goodbye in the entryway, she started to cry.

16th April 2017

I fell asleep on your grave on your seventy-second birthday. I fell asleep between the grass and the disappearing sunlight, your body and the sky. I brought you whisky and those 'round chocolates wrapped in gold foil', as you called them, then fell asleep but when I wake up you're still dead.

Daddy, I still don't know who else to talk to. You are the distance between me and other people. How long will I keep believing you will really come for me? How much is it possible to miss a person before you miss your whole life?

It's like there is something severed in me and though I can sense it, see it, know it is there, I can't reconnect it, can't reach the most essential part.

I'm in love with something you showed me and I am furious you have gone and left me seeing it. I wait for you, wait and wait. You are the edge of everything, the horizon, always moving away.

Why did you light me up like that just to leave me over and over again? Left here with all these strangers who don't believe in anything.

But it's right here in the way a pen moves across old paper, grass is so green, just exactly what we mean by green, everything is exactly as it is, and how long until I stop believing with certainty you're here?

Am I denying reality? But you shaped my reality. You created the metaphysical structure. I have no way out of you.

So beautiful, the way a pen moves across paper, thoughts leaving traces like a snail. I wait and wait and will I wait forever? Daddy, Daddy, Daddy, I miss you.

Where did you go?

I have made a companion of your deadness. I have made your death into my friend. Sun appears from behind a cloud and lays its warm hand on my head. I crave loneliness so I can be alone with you. I whisper to you across pavements littered with cigarette butts and gum and drunks in their pain and teenagers and babies, shoppers, robbers, mobile phones, bus stops and traffic lights and road markings and boredom in their pain, I whisper to you still believing you will come.

A plastic windmill twirls on your neighbour's grave. You are the space between me and other people. The things we talked about I won't talk about again. What

I loved in you is what I wait for, try to emulate, look for in the world and never find – the way the room lit up exactly when I walked in or you walked in and we saw what it was we could be for each other. But you're too big, you are all I can see, bigger than it is possible for a person to be, though I know you won't excuse my cut-out-and-keep version, how many parts of you I am eliding.

What I am talking about is not you but the way the sun comes out and the way the pen moves across the paper.

Time just goes on and on. It goes, and you don't go anywhere, though I sense you getting nearer and farther.

I read the long poem you wrote when you were just a year older than I am now, and all at once there was your voice, again, the way you broke apart and switched and connected up the world for me, again.

What does my brother long for of you? Does he find it in his girlfriend? Does he find it in his friends, in his aloneness? What am I looking for and how can I find it and when can I come home to you?

How much longer will I go on believing you are still coming home? How much longer will I go on waiting for some word from you?

I am furious with everyone for being nothing like you. For reducing the world to facts, anecdotes, jokes, for believing so firmly in science, in the fact of your death. I am not myself. I cannot be myself. There is too much which rests with you.

No, I can't ever say what I mean, there are no words for it. The way the pen moves across the paper, the way grass is so exactly green. It is always more than being alive.

There is a frisson, if you just rest your eyes. I can't stop looking and I need you to explain it to me, my lazy words aren't making their way.

Daddy.

All the things it was not possible to say. I knew nothing until you were dead and know nothing now, but the wind is cooler, the sky darkening, how can I summon the will to find the words to describe all this? The sun returns to warm my back: is this laziness, or am I afraid to fall short? I wish you were alive to spend a day writing an essay on this for me. You would've asked the ancient mystics like they were your old friends. You would have written it out in all your different-coloured pens. You had a quote or a poem for everything – I always believed age would make me like that but I'm too old now to hope you will spring from me like some butterfly from a chrysalis, it is not possible to believe such things.

But how much longer will I go on believing you will come for me? Have I got myself trapped in your dead head?

I'm sleepy, and I want just to talk to you. To fall into the space between me and other people. Close my eyes.

Sunlight again. This green, green grass. And the way the pen moves across the paper like a snail.

SSB's Dictionary

Turncoat: a person who rapidly changes their behaviour or values unrecognisably, either on one extreme occasion or back and forth repeatedly. Each side of the personality has little recollection of the other.

What happened?

You left.

I was born and you left. I was born in November and by the next March, you were gone.

But that's not quite right, is it?

You didn't leave, did you? You asked us to leave.

You asked my mother to move out, to take my brother and me to live somewhere else. I was four months old and he had just turned two. You had a poem to write. Your long poem on Nietzsche, *The Dream of Intelligence*. It was not a dream of childcare. It was not a dream that could be dreamed in a small flat in the company of your wife and two infants. You assured her that you had not broken up. It was only space you needed in order to finish your poem. My mother knew how much it meant to you. It was why you stayed up all night. It was why, when she was pregnant with me, you drove across East Germany in your clapped-out Avenger with a boot full of banned books. She had tracked your obsessions, your break-throughs, the expansion of the paper manuscript that, in its final form, filled over a metre of shelf space. She loved you. So she took your two children and moved out.

Kentish Town high street, March 1989, my mother pushing a rickety double buggy, shop to shop, asking for cardboard boxes to pack our things. She hired a van, carried the boxes herself, manoeuvring between the endless interruptions of my brother and me – feeding, sleeping, changing, holding, all the demands of young children you could not stand – to the flat up the road she would pay for with housing benefit. It hadn't been inhabited for several months, but after living with a furious poet, it seemed huge.

We had no furniture besides the table and chairs already there. You said you would build us some shelves. My mum's sister bought us a sofa bed and the three of us slept in it together in the bedroom upstairs, at street level. The room had a large window that looked over the drop to the basement below. The story my mum tells, of the first night we stayed there: the three of us were sleeping when in the middle of the night she woke up and opened her eyes to a pair of hands pushing open the window. Immediately she leapt up, shouting at whoever it was to get out. The intruder scrambled backwards, leapt across the gap and ran away. My mum stayed up, watching, the rest of the night.

Who was it? A burglar? A squatter? Perhaps someone who had been living there until that night? There were burglars, several times, later. The basement door was thin plywood and could be kicked through in one muffled boot. We never had anything expensive, but watched our hand-me-downs disappear within weeks of arrival: the TV, the VHS player, a camcorder loaned by the neighbours to record my third birthday, my mother's jewellery, her purse, her record player.

Where were you, while all those invisible strangers walked our belongings out of the door?

Two miles down the road, writing your poem.

Not only writing your poem.

We had lived without you two months when the four of us went to Greece together, my mother showing me, your Greek-named daughter, to all your friends there for the first time. I crawled on the waxed floor and rode in the yellow boat, tried to sneak sand into my mouth beneath my white cotton sunhat. My brother swung on the swing he was finally big enough for. You fixed a railing to the balcony so neither of us could fall off, as my brother had done the year before. But when we came back to London, you were gone again, and we were back in our home without you.

A few weeks later, unable to deny your coldness any longer, my mum rang you up and asked you: was there someone else?

You said, 'Yes.'

What changed in that moment? How much came undone? If this was the truth, why did you wait to be asked? These questions are my questions. I don't know what my mother said. I can only imagine what happened to each of us in that moment.

I know she drove there, back to the flat the two of you had so recently lived in together and, leaving my brother strapped in the back of the car, carried me in her arms and walked to the door. She rang the bell. She saw the curtains she had made drawn across her old bedroom window. She banged on the door. She called your name. But it wasn't you who answered, was it? It wasn't you who let her in. It was someone else. Your someone else.

Where were you? Not in the kitchen where she had prepared however many meals, not in the living room where she had chased my brother all over the floor. She came to the French windows that opened on to the garden and stopped. There you were, sitting at your desk on the grass under the roses she had planted that were just coming into bloom.

You looked at her, your face devoid of expression.

You didn't say a word.

I imagine you seeing her there.

I imagine her saying your name.

I imagine myself in her arms.

I imagine my view – the upside-down world, swaying trees, scattering pigeons, scrunched-up faces, tossed-out words. I imagine myself spinning and spinning. I imagine my mother's heart beating at my cheek.

I imagine your silence, your stillness. I imagine your refusal to feel guilt.

I imagine how she looked to you then, the betrayed woman, the abandoned mother, the same age I am now, a baby in her arms, what you called her *transcendental beauty*, and what had it got her? This:

Your slight shake of the head, glance down at your desk.

Your squint into the sunlight, grasp of your pen.

Your dull frown behind your glasses.

Your someone else's stare.

And all her insults, all her fury, all the truth she wanted to hurt your other woman with, all her pain slicing across the garden. All the things in the flat that were once hers that now she wanted to rip from the earth.

And me in her arms, beginning to grizzle, waltzing with her anger, beginning to scream, her upside-down face, upside-down fury like love somehow. I was her rocket, her shield, her proof of your love. I was her blood and your blood and the scar in her belly still healing from six months before. I was her child and your child and something undeniable and I was spinning in the hurricane of irresolvable grief.

Bright sunlight, that's how I picture it. One of those perfect, long summer days.

A glass of white wine beside your notebooks on the table. Roses blooming over you and your poetry. Your complex thoughts and polysyllabic words, your clean clothes and uninterrupted sleep. Your someone else. All these things that had nothing to do with us.

What happened?

She must have run out of words, run out of anger, run out of energy. She must have run out of the flat. Perhaps she remembered my brother in the car. Perhaps there was nothing left to say, nothing left to see. Perhaps some greater force within her led her out, away from your silence and the eyes of your someone else.

Years later, when I asked her about all this, she told me that she felt like she had been murdered.

Murdered.

And nobody investigating the crime.

A cover-up.

Your life continuing without us while she nursed your baby daughter and raised your son two miles up the road. It wasn't far to come and see us but still sometimes the distance was too hard for you to cross.

Our lives continued without you. I learned to talk and said my brother's name first. My mother made curtains for all our new home's windows to draw against the world and its intruders. You visited or you didn't. You went away and came back. You said you were still my mother's husband – and you were, legally, until 1991. Then, in 1998, you got married again and your someone else became your third wife. Eventually, we grew up.

Why did you do it? I still don't know.

The flat was too small or our needs were too big, your money ran out or the poem ran over everything, you yourself didn't know what dads were for. I know and I don't know. Perhaps I don't want to know. Perhaps it's so obvious something in me refuses to think it. Perhaps it doesn't matter any more.

But all the same, if I close my eyes and imagine, I'm

still there, six months old in my mother's arms, spinning and spinning through an upside-down world, both of you unreachable, pain matched with silence, longing twisted into hatred, that stranger's face in the middle of it, and the bright July sun rolling along the ground.

The scientist

A fter your operation, the second treatment offered to
you was radiotherapy. This would not remove the
tumour or even shrink it, the doctors kept reminding
us, but it might improve your quality of life. You were
dubious and so was I – what did 'quality of life' mean?
What chance was 'might'? But these weren't questions
it was possible to voice once it became clear that to the
others all they meant was hope. So if I started out
commiserating with you at the decision you faced, soon
I started to worry my feelings were all wrong.

When you rang me to tell me the treatment had been
scheduled for early September, you sounded optimistic.
Clearly, you had been persuaded.

I tried to copy your tone but a weight pressed through
me; a slow, burning feeling I did not want to name. After
we hung up I felt invaded by thoughts and questions
that distressed me. Didn't I want you to get better?
Didn't I want you to take every chance you had? Even
my brother, who I counted on being realistic, insisted
you might have years left. I assumed it must be my own
badness, a selfish desire to have the worst over with, that
stopped me feeling the same.

So although on the surface I joined our shared family

narrative of a future, underneath I was in turmoil, layering exhaustion with resentment and guilt.

And as if to draw attention to what I was hiding, the narrative soon began to shift and the radiotherapy became infused with magical properties. 'Might' meant certainty. 'Quality of life' meant that a dose of radiation could twist you back through time so that you could live out your terminal diagnosis in perfect health, stride across rooms with full lung power, make plans stretching years into the future. It was seductive, this new kind of phrasing, that life could be measured, optimised, extended. I could barely look your wife in the eye as she laid out all the dates and numbers and test results that were supposed to mean something like good. I was fearful of telling anyone how I felt in case they saw the same badness I did. Instead, I trawled cancer forums and conducted frantic Google searches looking for strangers who felt as I felt.

It took me years to forgive myself, to understand that it wasn't any cruelty in me, only desperation pushed up against a hard edge. I didn't want to see you in pain, to watch you crumbling, to watch you suffering and bored, tired of your diminished self. I didn't think you wanted that, either. I could not stand the oscillating possibilities, the back and forth between impending doom and regular, painful life. But much more than that, I wanted us to be honest so that we could be there with you, so that we would have a chance to say goodbye. I didn't want to pretend. There had been so much pretending in our relationship already and I was furious with whatever tides were forcing us to go on with it. That was why I felt only a leaden kind of peace when a gentle Scottish nurse on the Macmillan helpline told me no, if it was as I'd told her, radiotherapy or not, it wouldn't be long before you died.

Ih the end, there was no need to speculate. Of all the things that you had to endure, the radiotherapy would be the one we regretted the most.

For weeks afterwards, you were a dying man. To sit with you was to sit with a person dangling by a thread over a precipice. You were barely awake, and when you were awake you were in pain, and humiliated by it, alienated from your own body by the loss of taste and smell, the bitter exhaustion.

I came to see you every Sunday afternoon and on Wednesday mornings. Most of the time I was there, you were sleeping. You were in the bed in your study and I would sit in the large leather swivel chair at your desk, not wanting to sit too close to you in case it felt like an intrusion. I read the books on your shelf, either becoming so engrossed that I forgot where I was or not comprehending the words at all. When you woke up, it would take you several minutes to understand what was happening, what time or day it was, who I was. And I was supposed to persuade you to take handfuls of drugs that made you feel worse again, drink cartons of Ensure that made you feel sick, hold your arm so you could get out of bed and sit on the commode chair and wee into the bucket while I stood outside on the landing. With all your protestations, it felt as though we were torturing you – children who had captured a wild sea creature and kept it alive in a dank, bare bucket.

I thought you would die. I was sure of it.

The doctor had told you to take as much oramorph as you needed, and I deduced from this that this was the end, that you were so close to death that losing a few extra days of life by drinking too much morphine was preferable to the pain those days would entail.

By now my earlier tirade of feelings had condensed to a constant panic, breathless fear buffeting me from moment to moment. Whether I was at your house or not, you were always with me. I couldn't sleep or talk about anything else. I lay awake at night beside my boyfriend, my heart pounding, bothering him, or passed in and out of consciousness on my own, losing the ability to tell the difference between nightmare and life. I didn't know what I was saying. I started to feel as though people were afraid of me, that I was a scary thing to them. My mouth was full of ulcers and my bitten fingers were scabbed and raw. It was as though your death was contagious, visible in my flesh, making people leap away when I approached.

Why did you go along with it? Or were you pretending, as I tried to?

I kept thinking of you back in July, your brightness and philosophical acceptance of the whole thing, your gruff insistence on continuing to work, your film review email essays. It did not seem possible to me that you wanted this, that you wanted anything to do with these vague notions of 'quality of life'. The poet in you detested the phrase, the philosopher the idea, I felt sure of that.

But the poet and the philosopher weren't the only parts of you. You were also a scientist. You studied physiology at Oxford back in the sixties. Afterwards, you began a PhD in which you were your own test subject, experimenting with the effect of different drugs on the heart. Though you gave it up during the first year, you never lost your enthusiasm for the intricacies of atoms, cells, DNA, space–time, gravitational fields. You read *The New Scientist* and popular science books, often looking up the original papers behind them. Perhaps it was the scientist who made the decision – or at least who was willing to accept the decision that others made for him. It was the scientist who turned up that day at the hospital for the radiotherapy.

Born in April 1945, your life was concurrent with the development of medical applications of radioactivity. You had heard about the lasers, the hospital bed, the metre-thick lead door, seen photographs of them. For the scientist in you, the radiotherapy appointment was an extended, experiential field trip. Whatever misgivings you had could be outweighed by your curiosity for inspecting giant machines, complex physics translated into metal and screens and lab coats. And perhaps as far as it soothed your doubts, you wanted it to soothe mine too, because you chose me to accompany you to the hospital.

I hadn't been asked to any appointments before. Your wife always took you and my sister, who took charge of organising much of it, went along for support. So when you rang me to ask me to come along, I was touched. Of course I wanted to go. But more than that, I wanted to be asked. You said you thought I'd like to see the machine.

The day arrived and I walked from Whitechapel where I lived to the hospital at St Paul's, watching the sari stalls turn into curry houses and chicken shops and fancy coffee shops, the red-brick terraces turn into towering glass offices, before the sandstone grandeur of Bank and Monument and the brand-strewn high street behind St Paul's, all the way up to the hospital. I waited for you outside. Your car pulled up and I took your wheelchair out of the boot and helped you into it while your wife drove off to park. We waited, watching the traffic in the warm September sun, talking about the great machine, its power and magnificence, the unbelievable precision and modernity of the scientific model behind it.

When your wife returned, she led us inside. The radiotherapy department was down in the basement.

'It's one of several instruments of medicine that can also cause death and disease if not used correctly,' you explained as I wheeled you down the winding ramp. You were talking to the air in front of you, gesticulating, a lecturer giving a tour. Your thick hair was dirty, combed into silvery strands over your scalp that I had become too familiar with during the past few months.

The doctor met us downstairs and after he greeted us, you continued explaining. You had met the doctor before, when you came for a consultation, and from the expression on his face and slow gait, leaning in to catch your words, I understood he was charmed by you. He told me that, yes, my dad was right in everything he was saying, at which point you assured the doctor that I didn't need either of you to explain the machine to me.

'She has a degree in physics from Leeds University,' you told him, pushing the truth to its limit, as usual. 'But I wanted her to see how it works in practice. To see the theory come to life.'

We modulated our fear with knowledge, and in sharing our knowledge we shared our vulnerability, and this made the intimacy of the day into something bearable, the coldness and sadness of the basement, the lasers, the word *palliative*, into a connection between us. We talked about subatomic particles and the Hadron Collider, their newness and unwieldiness, how tiny and invisible and impossibly powerful they were, right there in the atoms in the cells that made up everything including our bodies. Then it wasn't my dying dad being wheeled into a basement for a treatment that wouldn't change anything, but an outing we'd organised, an object lesson in particle physics.

The doctor humoured us. You had been here before but he let you show me around before you got changed, smacking your palms on both sides of the metre-thick door, waving an arm over the wall of buttons and screens in the control room, insisting I wheeled you right up to the bed you would lie on to inspect the giant laser that would be aimed at your chest.

'One point five million pounds, this machine costs,' you told me. 'And just the short dose they will give me today costs the NHS tens of thousands.' You were nodding at me over your glasses, your eyebrows raised, encouraging me to marvel not only at the technology, but the wonder of the healthcare system. 'A gift to the country after the travesties of the Second World War. Do you know how many people died of the flu, and how many more were at death's door? My father, your grandfather, was one of them, and he never forgot it after.' You explained that you would be strapped down so that you could not move, since it was of the utmost importance that the laser touched only a specific part of your chest. 'So important, in fact,' you told me, 'that they gave me my first ever tattoo,' and pulling down the neck of your T-shirt, you showed me the single black dot on your chest.

I blinked at it, this tiny black dot, the size of a 12pt 'O' filled in. I knew from showing you my own tattoos that you hated the idea of permanent ink on the body, and for a moment I could not maintain the student's detached curiosity but felt devastated. To me, that dot didn't mean accuracy, medical efficiency, physics, precision, technology. It didn't even mean cancer. What that tattoo meant at that moment: your body didn't matter any more.

I tried to regain my brightness, but I couldn't get my expressions, my voice and my thoughts to match up.

Perhaps you picked up on this, or perhaps you felt the same – the field-trip aura fading like the atmosphere in a cinema after the lights have been switched on – because back in the changing room, where your wife was waiting, you were old again, very old and tired and sad. She helped you take off your shirt and I tried not to look, not to see the liver spots on your back, the collapsed skin, the cragginess of the bones in your arms and shoulders. You put on your hospital gown, faded and crisp, before taking off your trousers and shoes. The last thing you took off was your necklace.

It was then you turned to me, looking straight at me for the first time since I had greeted you at the car outside. 'Here,' you said. 'You can look after this. Don't lose it. It's extremely precious.'

I didn't need you to tell me that. I knew exactly how precious it was and you knew that I did. I knew also that it wasn't for the obvious reasons that you said this. I fastened it around my neck.

'Good idea,' you said, your eyes tracking my fingers

on the clasp. It was the twin of the necklace I had on already, and your eyes narrowed, taking in the sight of them together.

Then the doctor said it was time to go.

Your wife gave me a look that meant I should go with you, taking your arm to help you walk into the room. She and the doctor walked on your other side. We helped you on to the bed. A technician lowered it so you could climb up before raising it again. You lay down. The doctor strapped you in.

The straps disturbed me – the unavoidable suggestion of struggle, refusal, punishment. I chewed my mouth not to say anything. I knew I was liable to make bad jokes in situations like this. I kissed your cheek for good luck, as did your wife, and you looked up through your eyebrows to say goodbye, because you couldn't move your head.

The doctor said it would be better if we left now so he could get everything right.

We waited in the other room, the control room, standing behind the technicians at the screens with their buttons and levers. The two of them looked like pilots as they aimed the invisible laser at a few square millimetres on your chest. One of them pressed a button and, in pixellated black and white, we watched the thick lead door close. That door was there for us, not you. It was to keep us safe while you lay in the danger zone, quarantined with your cancer, however many of your healthy cells in line to be sacrificed under the ray of the ionising particles. And in so many ways that was what this treatment meant – your future had become expendable.

Between the pads of my thumb and forefinger I pressed the silver ichthus pendant on your necklace. A Greek Christian symbol of a fish – in this case, two fish swimming into each other – it had been hanging around your neck since before I was born. Ichthus. The name is an acronym, you had shown me once, the letters in Greek stand for Jesus Christ, Son of God, saviour. My mum has the same necklace. She got hers when you got married and had given me my own more recently, for my twentieth birthday. My brother had one from his baptism, though he never wore it. It was one of the anomalies of our disbanded family, that we all still had the same necklace. I ran the two ichthuses together along their separate chains, ran them over my chin, my bottom lip, feeling the metal getting warm and the bumpy glide of the clasp over the chain, looking and trying not to look at you and all the masterstrokes of modern technology, your stillness around your almost imperceptible breathing, your eyes staring at the ceiling, knowing we were watching, perhaps, but unable to look back at us.

What came to my mind was a line from your poem – 'death is a stealth bomber /under the roof of our radar'. I wondered if while you were lying there you were thinking this too, whether or not you were willing the radioactive attacks of these doctor-pilots to win the battle, whether or not you could abide your own words any more, and who was alive in you now: the scientist, the poet, the mystic philosopher staring into the mouth of death, or just an old man alone in a room wondering how much longer he had left to wait.

SSB's Dictionary

Heideggerian mistake: a catastrophic error in judgement brought about by hyperfocus on one idea at the cost of ignoring others.

Hangover

You never got hangovers, did you?

You drank regularly and compulsively during my lifetime and before, but I never saw or heard you complain of being hung-over. My mother taught us, growing up, not to call you after six in the evening because you'd be drunk, but we did sometimes, and she was right. You'd slur and say strange things and either not remember or we'd get a phone call the next day to confirm whatever plans we'd made. Sometimes you'd be unkind or dismissive and say goodbye quickly, or just hang up. Other times I'd welcome your warmth and enthusiasm, the emotion I could detect in your voice. You drank red wine, mostly, but also vodka, tall glasses topped up with a splash of orange juice, or whisky, straight, no ice. You drank white wine in summer and rosé too, said you always thought rosé was cheap but going to the South of France with your wife every summer you learned its true sophistication. 'Sophistication,' you always said, 'is wisdom on rollerskates.'

There is wine all through your poetry, sometimes particular grapes mentioned by name, and there is the obvious haze of alcohol at work in several too. One of my favourite poems gives a pretty accurate image of what you were like to be around at exactly the right point in the evening – generous, expansive, slightly melodramatic, a person in the grip of something more powerful than wine. It's called 'Under the Elderberry Tree'. These are excerpts:

> It is so appalling
> Not to be drunk
> While the blackbird is singing
> And the stars penetrate the sunbeam
> In the orchards of paradise.

Or:

> Drunk again,
> The Milky Way
> Cascades on my page.

In fact, the whole second part of this poem, subtitled 'In Bashō's Hut', reads like a wine-fuelled vision of the seventeenth-century Japanese poet, Matsuo Bashō, and his philosophy of numinosity and interdependence. I understand that it is not only wine you are drunk on, that there is metaphorical as well as literal meaning, but one doesn't cancel out the other.

Were you addicted to alcohol or to these alcohol-born mystic experiences?

The latter, I can imagine you saying, but addiction would not be your word, and nor can I swallow the distinction.

Almost everyone dependent on alcohol has a reason they're not an alcoholic.

Different questions: did you need wine to write poetry? Does that change the fact you depended on both to survive?

I'm no good at drinking alcohol, though there was a time when I wanted to be. Like you I am a lightweight. Two strong beers and I don't know what I'm saying. A bottle of wine and the evening is blanked out. I drink vodka soda, down pints of water in between, try to skip rounds without anybody noticing. But sometimes I want to get drunk. Sometimes I do. Then either I am very good company, chatting to strangers and finding fun in everything, or else something happens and I capsize into a sea of shadows in which every word spoken is criticism, my friends hate me, I am boring everybody, I am exhausted and want to lie down. I don't know if the amount of alcohol consumed is directly proportional to how unhappy it makes me, or if it's drinking when unhappy that leads to going overboard, but these days it feels easier to drink less, regardless.

Unlike you, I get hangovers, and they're excruciating.

From around the age of fourteen most of the people I knew had started drinking. The parties we went to would undoubtedly involve alcohol – crates of alcopops or beer bought by older siblings or measures of spirits siphoned off parents' supplies. Later we had fake IDs to buy our own cheap corner-shop wine or lager to take to parties or drink in the queues for indie clubs the same fake IDs got us into. I never questioned the necessity of drinking, in fact I embraced it. I didn't like school and this felt not only easier but realer, more important. Wasn't that what you and Bruce Springsteen had told me?

I would never say that I drank because of you. That would not be correct. But when I found myself in a world of drinking, I knew that you were the kind of drinker I wanted to be. Not the vacant man slurring about sixteen white stallions, but the younger version, the person I had met only in anecdotes. The one who came from a family of infamous bohemians whose lives, according to the stories you told me, seemed to consist entirely of drunken revelations, wild parties and charming irreverence. For example, the one about your mother, Elizabeth Smart, how one night in Toronto just before she died she went out with a group of her young colleagues and students until two in the morning. They were walking to another bar when she threw herself down on the pavement and refused to get up, shouting, 'Don't you know I'm seventy-two years old!' It seemed to me then that drunkenness was equivalent to freedom from convention, a kind of truthful insouciance. It almost felt like it was a form of creativity.

That's how it felt, when it was good – like something productive, a way to be more than myself. It took away the feeling of embarrassed shyness that had prickled all over my skin ever since I could remember. It took away the continuous tirade of shame I felt about my changing adolescent body. It was a way to make friends, to have the kind of intense, intimate conversations I was always looking for, that seemed to me the whole purpose of being alive. It was a potion to dissolve the boundaries between people that made me feel so alone the rest of the time. You used to say that you liked to dance as though your feet didn't touch the ground, like you were dancing on air, and that was what I was always looking for – weightlessness, the feeling of leaving my own body, to drink enough that I could see and hear and laugh and speak but not feel I was there.

These were the things I would have told you about – the music, the conversations, all the dancing – wanting to prove that my life, my generation was interesting too. But there were other things – things I wouldn't have told you. Things I tried not to think too much about. Losing my phone, my address, my memory. Breaking my hand, my elbow, slicing open my shin, chipping one tooth and then another. Fights with friends, boyfriends, bouncers, strangers. Falling asleep in the wrong place, going home with the wrong person, saying the wrong thing at the wrong time. It was not hard sometimes, though not comfortable either, to recognise in myself my own sixteen white stallions, though I was never as good at forgetting as you. Instead, I did what so many of my friends did also, turning anything awkward or painful into a funny story to tell the next day. That is, once anyone else was awake. Like you, I would be wide awake before anybody else, but for me this meant being blasted at 5 a.m. by an internal monologue screaming every iteration of anxiety, not sure if I was about to have a heart attack or be sick. The feeling would last all day, sometimes several days, sometimes it didn't feel like it stopped at all. My hangovers were so bad I tried several times to stop drinking, but my will never lasted beyond the next night out.

But there were other things that happened which weren't so easy to brush off.

I had been groped or kissed against my will enough times to be generally wary of men, especially drunk ones. If I ever walked home alone I would be wide-eyed, vigilant, my keys gripped as claws between my fingers, my phone in one hand ready to call for help, my drunk brain whirling with all the worst things I imagined could happen, all the things I would be ready to do. But in the end when the worst thing happened I didn't react in any way I expected or understood. It didn't look like I thought it would, either. It felt like a huge thing and it felt like nothing and I wanted it to disappear so I could get on with my life.

But it wouldn't disappear. It wouldn't stay folded away in my rationalising mind. I kept remembering, thinking about it. And my body would not shut up. I felt sick and uncertain most of the time, as though my edges had all been punctured. I had nightmares and night terrors, especially if there was someone else in the bed. I began to question other things that had happened, things I was no longer sure of. It was as though the lens I was looking at the world through had been changed, and it was hard to make sense of my earlier self at all. I didn't want to see many people, or to go out to any of the places I used to go. I didn't want to get drunk. I didn't particularly want to be sober around drunk people, either. At twenty-two, these felt like lonely decisions. I would listen to my housemates getting ready, chatting and laughing, getting louder and drunker and finally leaving the house, waiting for the kitchen to be empty so I could make tea without making anyone uncomfortable, wondering how I used to have the energy for all that. I didn't know if I was miserable or the calmest I'd ever been. I drank herbal tea and went to bed early and couldn't sleep, lay there worrying instead until long past my housemates got home. I knew there were things I needed to process, I just had no idea how to do that.

If writing for you was a way to escape yourself, to transcend your own needs, your body, your emotions, for me it was a way to be still so that I could understand them. All the empty space not drinking left behind I started to fill with writing – and all the things I had not thought about in years, I began to figure out by writing them down. It was something to get up for, something to go to bed for, something to escape into when I was upset.

Apart from everything else, I'd been struggling with an eating disorder since I was thirteen and this, finally, felt like a chance to move beyond it. When I was drinking, when I was drunk, my body ruled itself – it demanded food, cigarettes, company, sleep, and I couldn't refuse it. When I was hung-over, too, there was always a sense of disembodiment, the shaking anxiety and sickness, the looming guilt that meant all my decisions were geared towards reparation. But sober, particularly after an extended period, my body felt like my own. And in this new, gentler habitation, emotions were no longer terrifying, but could be questioned, welcomed, wondered about.

There is only one poem of yours I can think of where you noticeably acknowledge your physical existence. It was a shock, when I first read it, only a couple of months before you died, to find myself inside your head, observing yourself and the marks of your ageing. You didn't know you were dying when you wrote it – sometime in the six or so years before – though I understood why most people assumed you did.

Autobiography

I waded in the shallows, watching sticklebacks.
Later, at school, I learnt how to compose
Sticklebacks out of words and numbers
To set them free in the river of my mind.

Later, the oceanography of water
Came in handy, as I sailed
The world, a water-boatman on the globe
Of unfathomable reason.

The world, too true, was tricky,
But the one inside me more so.
So I drank the wine of oblivion,
A familiar face in every port.

One day, in the mirror, I saw myself,
A composition of words and numbers,
Broken blood vessels and grey hairs.
So I said to myself, it's time to be off.

And out on the long river of my mind
I sailed to you in the tremendous
Oceanography of the sea
Outside myself, you graced the quay at dawn.

I guess you know by now if you found what you were looking for.

About eighteen months after you died, your wife arranged a memorial. Friends from every part of your life were invited to read or share memories. Afterwards there was a drinks reception. There were people I'd never met, people I'd never heard of, and I went around asking all of them for stories about you. I was in a good mood, feeling frivolous and extroverted, buoyed by the chance to spend the evening unapologetically talking about you.

I got into conversation with a friend of yours I knew reasonably well. She noticed I wasn't drinking and asked why.

I smiled and said, 'It makes me so depressed and anxious I can't do anything for days.'

She baulked at my frankness but after a moment she said, 'Well, that's hardly fair. Your dad never got hangovers at all. It used to drive us crazy when we were young.'

Apparently, you would be up in the morning making breakfast and looking fresh while your friends groaned and crawled to the toilet. I told her that was exactly what you were like when you took us to Greece as children. You'd get so drunk at night that you forgot we were there but in the morning – nothing. You'd be up before us in your clean clothes, singing along in your tuneless gravel voice to Maria Callas, drinking coffee and condensed milk from a tiny cup.

Hangovers, consequences, these were of no importance to you. 'I have no regrets,' you used to say. Then with a glint in your eye, you'd add, 'Except not learning Greek when I was in school.'

You said that often. As you got older, it was one of your favourite lines. It hurt me, every time you said it. What about leaving us? What about not seeing us? What about my mother? It seemed so unfair when, at twenty-two, I already felt overwhelmed by consequences. And yet if I'd thought about it long enough, I would have remembered you yourself had told me that the opposite was also true.

It's one of my most distinct memories of you, and the only time I can remember that you came close to suggesting this – that your boundless beatitude might be only an act, but one you relied on to protect yourself from realities you could not bear. It was an evening when I had to switch around and start again with all my different versions of you, and I loved you afterwards in a new way.

Do you remember that trip, in the spring of 2008, when I came to visit you alone in Greece? I hadn't stayed anywhere with you on my own before. It was just after you'd been forced to resign as editor of *The London Magazine* and you had begun to retreat into yourself, to lose an energy that never came back.

You were out in Greece for three weeks and I went to visit you. By day we drove all over the south-west Peloponnese and you told me about the Messenian Wars, the Dorians, the Venetian invasions, the Civil War – the same history you'd been telling me since I was a child. I made us sandwiches from out-of-date canned vegetables and soft papery bread and wrapped them in tin foil so we could eat them off our knees, leaning on the front of our twenty-five-year-old Lada. At about five o'clock we'd get home and you'd pull the two metal tables together and pour us both a three-inch measure of vodka, topped up with orange juice. You said it was how your mother liked it. You'd gulp yours and I'd sip mine, and your eyes would sink into their sockets. You'd talk about your mother being here, my mother being here, whatever else you happened to remember. Without my brother to insist on it, there'd be no barbecue, no home-made chips.

Part of the reason I had come, unknown to you, was to escape a particularly bad phase of bulimia, so I was grateful for the empty cupboards. I'd cut us more papery bread and slop tinned gherkins and olives and oily peppers on to plates, cut cubes of feta, fry slices of Spam, tease you about your taste for food from an era of ration books. When I sat down to eat, you'd ask every time how I got to be such an excellent cook, and you weren't teasing, you actually appreciated the effort. You knew how to be grateful for things. I ate deliberately and you drank heavily, quickly moving on to the thin, sour red wine, your stories rolling into each other.

All through the trip we were careful of each other, navigating the unfamiliar domesticity with our shared instinct for privacy, silence, subjects we would never venture on to. I felt that this was something you appreci-ated about me, as it was something I appreciated about being alone with you. We were at ease in our uneasiness, relieved to be granted the freedom not to be questioned too closely. Though I'd shared rooms, beds and baths with them my entire life, I did not feel so at ease with my mother and brother; they looked, they cared, so I had to hide. I thought that this would be how the trip ran, how it would end: the two of us quietly coexisting, talking around the things we most wanted to say. Sharing wine and stories and history instead of our feelings. But I had underestimated you again. Where I had seen coldness in you, there was something murkier, indistinct even to yourself.

It was the fourth night, the penultimate of my visit. I had cleared our plates and was doing the washing-up when you paused in the middle of the story you were telling to watch me, your head tilted. I can still feel the way my muscles moved at the sink, my teenage shyness, your adult gravity, the tension and awkwardness between us. We didn't really know each other, especially in the evening, over dinner, alone. You always were a master of these moments, the theatre of pedagogy, but this might be the finest I remember.

'Xanthi! I have something to tell you.' You turned your creaky wooden chair towards me, your hand raised, gesturing like the poet-professor you had once again become. 'You've just reminded me,' you said. 'I have thought about this for a long time. I have thought about this – the washing-up – and do you know what?'

I shook my head.

'Do you remember? A long time ago, when we were here, and you were very small, you were sitting right there on the bed and you were bored. You wanted to go out and do something. Your brother was off somewhere and I was doing the washing-up, washing up our breakfast things, and you said, "Daddy, don't you know there are more important things in life than the washing-up?" And I thought, I'll be damned, you were absolutely right. I thought it was the wisest thing anyone had ever said to me. I thought you were the wisest child in the world. So I stopped right there and off we went. And you were so pleased, you were delighted.'

I told you that yes, I remembered.

Then you shook your head and continued. 'What I think is – what I have come to understand is – you were wrong. I always thought you were right but you were wrong. Listen carefully. There is nothing – nothing – more important in life than the washing-up. I was wrong,' you said again.

Then you shook your head once more, as though to shake something out of it, and I saw behind your glasses you were crying. Tears rolling down your face.

Tears I had seen before – you cried with pride and joy quite often, in the cinema, at our school plays if you turned up, reading poetry, looking at the night sky. You loved to cry. You were always so moved by things. But this was a different kind of crying. You didn't intend it. You didn't want it. It was painful – and painful to watch. This lesson was a different kind of lesson, one you were not only teaching but learning yourself.

You were crying with regret.

Even I knew that. Nineteen years old and mostly concerned with music, boys, my friends, trying to eat as little as possible while going out as much as possible. But I knew what regret looked like. My mother had primed me. My mother who had always done the washing-up.

After a long time you said my name. Your tone was different, almost childlike. You told me your wife had given you your Native American name, a name that described you, like He-who-falls-like-an-eagle, or Sitting Bull.

I nodded to show I understood.

Then you asked if I knew what your name was.

I shook my head.

You shook your head. Then you told me. 'She said I would be He-who-has-read-all-the-books.' You let the name resound around the room. You let it sink in, what it meant, gave me time to appreciate it.

I thought you were telling me with pride. It was something many people would have been proud of.

But you said, 'I don't want to be that. I don't want to be He-who-has-read-all-the-books.'

'No?'

'No. No, I can see it now, who I should have been, who I might have been. Not He-who-has-read-all-the-books, but He-who-dances-in-the-light.'

I didn't know what to say then.

You cried and shook your head. You said you'd got it all wrong. You said you'd thought there were more important things in life than the washing-up, but there weren't. There was nothing more important than the washing-up. You said it over and over again. 'Xanthi,' you said, 'listen. There is nothing. More important. In life. Than the washing-up.'

You were not the poet-professor any more. Your eyes weren't sparkling and your hands weren't gesturing. Your gaze was fixed on the floor and you were gripping your knees.

I looked at you, surrounded by the house you had built, the poems on the walls and the crucifix above the door and the chimney that coughed all the smoke back into the room. The house you had built to write a poem in. The house you had built for the sake of all those books. I was waiting for you to look up, waiting for that big froggy smile that would sweep away feelings like this. I had almost finished the washing-up.

I said, 'Okay.'

I thought about my mother. I thought about the washing-up. I felt sorry for you and didn't want to. To stop the crush of feelings, I asked you what my name would be. You told me, but I don't remember what you said. I wish I did. But there was so much wine and vodka, and my dad crying, dog drunk, half blind, stumbling up, muttering that it was time to go outside.

But I wouldn't let you go this time. I followed you. I dragged another chair to where yours was at the edge of the balcony. I sat beside you under the vine-drenched trellis and we looked out over the plains and the black sky with its starry soup of constellations and you nodded and drank the wine you had brought out with us. I watched you out of the corner of my eye. You didn't look at me. We looked up and you nodded and cried and said something about your sister, your mother, your father, all your dead ones, and I wished I had known them and I wished you would tell me about them and I wished I could see into your head. You cried and I watched you and watched the sky and then I got cold and scared and you kept crying and crying and didn't say anything.

At last I said, 'Daddy, I think I'll go to bed.'

You looked at me, face flashing back to normal, and said, 'Okay.' Tipped your tumbler of wine at me, ducked your head.

I went inside and shut the door and put on an ancient scratchy tape of Pink Floyd and danced until I was exhausted enough to sleep.

In my dreams, you're often crying. It terrifies me. I can't stand it. The thought that the masks you wore were even flimsier than I imagined, that you were hurting underneath all that time, wanting to be found but nobody seeking you, that you could not believe we let you go on with your facade. This battle in my head between anger and pity, disbelief and nauseating understanding, evidence I didn't want to put together. All the things you'd wanted that had not appeared, and now you'd given up on them you saw they weren't the right ones after all.

Life had been too much. Now it was over.

*

The final straw was a few years later, when you were out in Greece with your wife and hurt yourself. You'd been sitting outside alone late in the evening. Your wife had already gone to bed. When you came inside, you caught your bare foot on the electric heater, and ripped the nail and a chunk of skin out of your right big toe. You didn't realise you'd done it until the morning, when you woke up to find the sheets covered in blood. You went to the pharmacist, who gave you some antiseptic cream for it, but then it started to go black. It swelled and burned. It had a bad smell. You came back to London and rushed to the doctor, who dosed you with strong antibiotics, hospital-grade bandages and a scolding. Another day or two and you might have lost it. Your hip replacement, scheduled for later that month, was postponed until the wound had healed.

You were shaken. I had never seen you shaken like that. You were deeply upset by it. You no longer wanted to go to the house. You sank into your oldness, your ageing body, lowered gaze. You shivered in your big coat, your hands retreating into the sleeves, even in the early summer heatwave. You had lost your night vision, you said, with a helplessness that once would have been charming but that now, without that laugh behind your eyes, suggested a child's desperation faced with the bleak, dark evening of your life.

I worried about you. I had just stopped drinking myself and was feeling lost and doubtful, almost skinless, but it felt unbearable to sense the same things in you. I missed your grandiose delusions. I wanted to help, though it was hard to get near you. You didn't want to see anyone, let alone talk about it. I was adamant you should return to the house. It wasn't right that after so long you should be scared away by your big toe and an electric heater. But that July you had your hip replacement, and by the time you recovered you had been diagnosed with cancer, so in the end you never got the chance. It always makes me sad to think that you didn't say goodbye to the house you built and loved for so long, but fled it in physical pain and mental anguish.

Were your final years one protracted hangover, all the hangovers you never had, added together and delivered in one? And if so, should I see myself as lucky to have found a reason to stop so early, to find another way to survive? Daddy, there are so many differences between us.

The 'wine of oblivion', that's what you called it in your poem. It wasn't until the days after you died that I understood how you must have used it as medicine, a kind of reckless balm that took the shape out of pain, turned the volume down. For two weeks, I took up your practice and turned the evenings into a watery blur of voices and faces. I hadn't drunk like that in years, hadn't felt so grateful to lose the boundaries between feelings, objects, words, people in years. But I could not sit alone like you, waiting for a vision, I wanted someone to talk to.

I remember complaining to you once, when I was about twenty-three, that my then-boyfriend wouldn't talk about his feelings.

You laughed as though the suggestion was absurd. 'Talk about his feelings!' you said. 'Of course he can't do that. He's a young man. There was a time when I'd rather have broken both my legs than talk about my feelings.'

Your reaction surprised me. In fact, it changed my understanding of you entirely. I hadn't thought of you as someone who didn't talk about his feelings: you were a poet! Didn't poets live for feelings? More than that, you were magical to me. I couldn't see your limitations. If I ever pictured you as a young man, it was as the young man I most wanted to meet. I understood you had flaws – you had left us, you were often indifferent, sometimes cruel – but I saw these as mistakes made by a perfectly functioning person, not as the inevitable failings of a person only half there, someone so splintered, perhaps, inside, that mistakes, cruelties, indifference were unavoidable, structural necessities too dangerous to acknowledge.

You'd grown up in a chaos you always described as idyllic, but stories I've heard protest otherwise. At home there was poverty, an endless stream of artist visitors, your mother coming and going. Then at seven you were sent to boarding school where your education and induction to upper-class societal norms were offset against the violence and abuse you witnessed there, that you could describe only in hushed fragments. I wonder sometimes what I expected of you, to father me in a way you'd never experienced or seen. In this wilderness of contradictions, it would have made sense for you to circumnavigate your feelings, to watch them from afar until they became abstract, inconsequential. Your poetry, perhaps, decades later, became the perfect vessel for these emotions to reemerge, purged of their every-dayness, the nuance that would have made them (too) personal: the child's sensibility returned, having escaped its vulnerability. In your poetry there is wonder, bafflement, horror, devastation, ecstasy, but as an adult I see that there is little of the small-scale feeling that exists between people, that makes up so much of the fabric of relationships and experience. This was exactly the kind of poetry you despised, in fact, like Larkin, who you dismissed as banal.

You didn't like everyday life, that's the crux of it. Alcohol was another way to escape it. The moments you wanted to witness, to record and to experience were those that transcended it. 'The tragedy of the everyday' – that's what you call it in your journal – the transcendent element to experience that is always there if you can attune to it. You wanted always to be attuned to it, not to be dragged into the tawdriness of the mundane. I can understand that, the fear of boredom, the instinct to make it otherwise. I want every day to be remarkable, even if what is remarkable is the way fingers tie shoelaces, or the way water spurts from a tap. I want things to be dramatic and emotionally raw at all times. I want each moment I share with someone to be absolutely intimate, with no disjointed feelings, no dislike, disregard or disagreement. I used to cry sometimes as a child out of boredom, and my mother would say, 'That's just what your dad was like.'

But I can see also that it's this drive to intensity that causes so many problems. It is all-consuming; you need to be constantly present, attentive to others and to the world around you, to let yourself be affected by everything. When I am tired and lack the strength for this, I feel despairing. When I'm ill, the tiredness and fogginess can quickly tip over into self-hatred and depression. And when I drink alcohol – which I do now with some-what more moderation – and for a few hours lose the will or the desire to try so hard, I still wake up in the morning terrified of what my unguarded self has done, what cringing banality I have committed. I am embarrassed by my ordinariness. It feels like a terrible shame to just be a person, as though to relax, to stop trying so hard, is to let others down irreparably.

But the farther I get away from you the less power you have, the freer I feel to disappoint you – and not only that, but the more I wonder whether the you I imagine is not you at all, only a distorted image, a force field of judgement I invented myself. I don't have to become you to stop you disappearing from the world.

So I'm trying not to try so hard. I'm trying to enjoy the boring things, not for some special quality but for their dullness. Because I wonder, thinking about you, Daddy, how much of the world you blocked out. How much did you refuse to look at because it was not magic, not transcendent, not something you could turn into poetry? How many evenings did you lose because you drank your way through them?

I remember the outrage I felt when I first discovered your phrase 'the tragedy of the everyday' in your journals. From what I understood, you meant it to denote something like the sublime loss signified in every moment, necessarily, because of its finitude. It was in a passage justifying your separation from my mother. She wasn't, you said, someone who could appreciate 'the tragedy of the everyday'. She was ordinary. A 'perfectly ordinary human being', you called her, which was fine, you said, but not compatible with your way of life.

You were dead when I read those words, but I wanted to tear the page out and demand an explanation. What could be a more everyday tragedy than a man leaving his wife and babies for another woman? It was boring, what you did. There was nothing transcendent about it. But what made me so angry was that I understood what you meant. I could see that to you our lives must have looked excruciatingly ordinary. Yet I also know what an achievement that was. In as far as our childhood was routine, my mother had succeeded in making it so. The unboring parts – the car so old it went up in flames with us inside it, the abrupt moves when landlords increased the rent, the boyfriends who came and went, my mother's sadness – were not the ones to be sought after.

But it was what I longed for, wasn't it?

To be bored with you, bored by you, to feel all right being boring around you. To do the washing-up with you. The most important thing in life, you said, in those pain-heavy days in 2008, when all your hangovers came at once. I felt sorry for you then, for what you'd lost, and for all the boring days of our lives you'd missed. What a wonder it would have been for all of us, for you to do the washing-up, your hands sunk in water, sponge scrubbing old food off dishes, TV on in the background, half-thoughts flitting across your head. And for you to let it be only that, another dull domestic task, not the most important thing in life. Just life, another itchy, protracted second of it, going on and on inconsequentially, added to the next.

Will this house last forever?

1.

You didn't pack any shoes.

You were travelling in slippers and you didn't pack any shoes.

You had your leather bag and it was flopped over because there was nothing in it except copies of your new book, a selection of fine-liners, a can of SprayMount, two pairs of underpants and a wash bag (maroon with navy and yellow stripes, dull with grease and dirt, and inside it all your post-war essentials: Asda Basics toothbrush, a new tube of Euthymol, a Bic razor, a bar of anonymous grey soap, a flannel). Then at the last moment you added a photocopy of the next three days' schedules from the *Radio Times*.

I said, 'Daddy, aren't you taking any shoes?'

You looked at me like I'd suggested we take a limousine.

'Shoes? I hadn't thought of that.'

'What if you want to go outside? What if there's an emergency?'

You looked at me and I understood everything I was too stupid to know five seconds earlier. Then I made a face so we could both forget.

'What about clothes, then? You could use an extra set, at least.'

We were going away for four days.

You nodded and shuffled and said I was quite right and looked at your wife who rushed upstairs to find you some and I blushed in the cold hallway with my feet still in the shoes I hadn't taken off, considering how shoes are not a thing it occurs to a person they will no longer need.

Then I said, 'So this is where I learned to pack light.'

I wanted to make you laugh and I almost did. Your smile gave way but a second later you were clutching the table, gasping that you needed to sit down.

I held out my arm and you took it, patting my shoulder with your free hand to cancel out our shame, and I helped you into the green armchair in the next room where snail trails ran superhighways across the carpet. You sat down and your head fell forward so your chin hit your sternum as your eyes shut, concentrating on getting your breath back. Fluttering sounds came from your chest, like – and it would not have been unlike you – you were keeping a menagerie of birds inside.

You sat in that chair, your hips door-wide though you'd lost so much weight. Last year's pride at your slim figure turned to baggy clothes, child-size bowls of cereal, ice cream you wouldn't eat because you said it tasted like cement. But I would have said you were built out of cement. The hugeness of you never felt fat to me but somehow heroic, necessary for your gravity, the sign of the house you built out of rubble on a mountainside built into you. I thought that was what *Dad* meant: man made of hardwood, made to last forever. I thought you looked as stately and collected and wise as a man could, who had been told he might die any day.

Your wife came back downstairs with your extra clothes. She looked like she was tired of this and didn't want to be. You smiled at her like a little boy and I stood on the green carpet with its silver trails and wished there didn't have to be so many apologies.

'Ready?' she said.

I carried our bags to the car while your wife checked the map. We weren't going far, nowhere we couldn't get back from in a hurry, somewhere in Kent I kept forgetting the name of. I helped you step by step down the path and across the pavement.

'So strong,' you said, jostling my arm, after I'd heaved you into the passenger seat, though you said you wanted to ride in the back.

That had been your joy for the past three years, since you forgot how to drive one afternoon on a motorway, driving me back from university. I had been painfully hung-over, half asleep, and did not notice what was happening until I heard your eye-blazed muttering as we pulled into a service station. I didn't know how to drive either, so you bolstered yourself with a vending-machine coffee and we crept the rest of the way back, going less than fifty in the slow lane, the hazard lights flashing. After that you'd only drive on residential streets, routes you'd taken thousands of times before. You said it gave you vertigo. You liked to sit in the back seat instead, as though you had a chauffeur, you said. But today you were needed in the front.

I sat in the back watching the wisps of your grey hair through the headrest and got the route up on my phone just in case. We drove and your wife asked me about the masters course I had started that autumn. I told her I was reading Camus and she told me all about him while I tried to concentrate and felt sick.

The car quickly filled up with the smell of you and I was breathing through my mouth not to inhale it. It had been going on for weeks, this smell, since September, since the radiotherapy. You said you were showering but no one had the heart to tell you that whatever you were doing wasn't enough. The whole house smelled of you. This potent mix of sweat and breath and damp and mould and urine, it knocked us out. It clung to our clothes. I would go to see you and then carry you around all day. Except it wasn't you, not at all. You had never smelt like that. You were Old Spice, Imperial Leather soap, car engines, cut pine, sage, sometimes cigarettes and wine and whisky. You were turpentine, oil paints, hog-hair brushes. You were the yellow pages of old books, the untouched crisp pages of new ones. You were elderberry trees and spring air, the wax we used to polish the floor in the house you built, the smell of the sticky wood of that front door, Marmite.

The smell of your illness was unbearable. I opened the window and prayed the draught wouldn't kill you. The cold, wet English air. I stuck my nose out and inhaled. I said I felt car sick and then I felt embarrassed for you.

When we arrived, I got out first to carry our bags inside while you and your wife discussed logistics. The key had been left in the door, a heavy mortice key in proportions I'd only seen on television. The house was long and narrow, a bungalow. A bothy – *The* Bothy, it was called. You'd explained the name to me the week before, when your wife told us that she had booked the place. A small, remote hut used for shelter by labourers. This – the bothy, the drive, four days with you – was my twenty-fifth birthday present.

The front door opened at the centre to a dark, narrow hallway. To the left was the living room, a kitchen in one corner, everything in beige and brown, gilt-framed pictures of hunting scenes on the walls and small, square windows obscured by billowing curtains. To the right was a small room where I would sleep, heavy with varnished furniture and a high, quilted bed; then a bright white bathroom, and on the other side a larger bedroom with antlers on the wall and three ornate cupboards for your one set of clothes. It was cosy and dull and dated. I put our bags in the right rooms and realised it would be only the second time in my life I'd stayed somewhere alone with you.

The sky outside was grey and lidded and the sunlight wasn't enough to break through the windows, so I switched the lights on before coming back outside to get you. I took the wheelchair from the boot and clicked it back into shape, wheeling it to the passenger door so you could climb into it. I liked pushing you in it, and though I know you didn't like having to use it, I like to think you liked it when I pushed you because I made a game of it, acting your personal tour guide of this two-wheeled vehicle. You'd been using it since the radiotherapy, back in September. Two months had passed since then and you could get out of bed again but walking was still difficult. Your whole body shook with each step and three or four took the breath out of you.

I wheeled you to the door and you stood up and took my arm and said it always interested you to see the insides of new houses, while I worried you would miss the low step in the doorway.

'So strong,' you said again.

I delivered you to an upright wooden chair in the living room – you had always been suspicious of sofas – and went back to fetch your bag of drugs. This bag was heavier than your holdall.

'You're like Hunter S. Thompson,' I said.

You laughed and I put it down beside the fridge so I didn't have to see your face. I'd been trying to make you laugh all morning and now that it had happened, I regretted it immediately. It wasn't funny after all, to be going on a drugged-out trip with your daughter to the Kentish countryside in the middle of November with the very real chance you wouldn't come back.

I made your wife a hot chocolate and unpacked the food while she went over your medication schedule with us once more. There were drugs for pain and drugs for breathing and drugs to counteract the effects of the other drugs.

I'd asked you once what they all did and you smiled and said, 'Absolutely nothing. But she wants me to take them, so I do.'

She gave me a typed and printed copy of the schedule and I attached it to the fridge with a golf magnet.

After the hot chocolate and another look at the map, your wife left and we were alone. I made us sandwiches for lunch and you told me again about the history of bothies and then you sent me out to explore. I didn't go far – the little light there was left was fading – but it was nice to see the red, amber and yellow leaves, watch the sky turn pink through the trees, to climb over stones and abandoned houses and breathe clean air. There was a footpath that led through the woods, called Split Tree Lane on the map, and it did split the red forest in two like Moses, except with a cement builders' yard and a B road at the end.

When I got back it was almost dark. You were watching TV and I sat on the puffy sofa beside you. You were watching the news. It was fifty years to the day since JFK was shot and you told me how you were eighteen years old and in the middle of a rugby match when it happened, how they stopped the game to tell you. We watched the coverage on TV for almost three hours, in between fragments of cricket and rugby and the other headline news that three women had been kept as slaves in Britain by a sixty-seven-year-old couple for thirty years. I said how that must mean one of the women was born in captivity, and your mouth twisted up in disgust like it hurt you to know this and under your breath you repeated, 'Thirty years, thirty years.' I remembered that morning I'd looked at the books on your shelf, the spines bleached from sitting in the same place for decades, and thought about what thirty years can do and what it can't.

I asked if you wanted a cup of tea and you said yes, and I made it the way you thought was so special, using a pot and putting the milk in the cup first.

You asked if it was Lapsang Souchong.

'Yes,' I said. 'I bought some especially.'

'And you put honey in it?'

I nodded.

You inhaled the steam, thanked me again and said I had my mother's knack for making tea. It was thirty years also, you said, since you first met her.

Around seven you were hungry so I cooked us spaghetti, filling my own plate mostly with tomato sauce, and you told your wife on the phone we were having a great time. I thought perhaps we were. The booze had been packed in the medicine bag – Hunter S. Thompson was closer than I thought – and you'd drunk three glasses of wine and lost the shake from your voice. I was sitting beside you on the sofa eating handfuls of peanuts feeling like we were two young men in an eighties sitcom. You kept topping up my first glass so it remained full while yours kept emptying.

When I got up to do the washing-up, you asked for another bottle and I hesitated. Your wife had left no instructions for your favourite drug. I could see the fade in your eyes but I didn't want to disappoint you. When I'd questioned you, months ago, if it was all right for you to drink with all the morphine you were taking, you'd said, 'Yes, of course, Xanthi – the two have been taken together for centuries. It's what the Victorians used to call laudanum.' I thought tonight you must have caught my hesitation because you said you'd had enough for now. Then I came back to sit down and saw you'd poured us both a glass of whisky.

After all your stories about JFK you weren't saying much and this bothered me. I'd never sat with you and had nothing to say. You always had something to say. I tried to think of something to ask you, something to tell you. I worried I was an inadequate companion. The paid work I did was uninteresting to me, there was no way I would have bored you with that. The masters course I had started was in comparative literature, and ostensibly part of the rationale for this trip was that we would be able to talk about some of the books I was reading. But the books I was reading had recently proved problematic.

For example, we were studying *Death in Venice*. To my shame, I'd given you a copy a few weeks earlier when you told me you needed something to read. You told me you were reading Sherlock Holmes, had a newfound passion for Arthur Conan Doyle – his meticulous crafting, satisfying narratives, historic detail, sleuths and villains. You said reading was the one thing you could do, your sole pleasure because you couldn't write. But you didn't want to read the things you usually read. You didn't want to read theological poetry. You didn't want to read dense religious texts, political commentary, couldn't look at any literary reviews. You asked me to bring you something to read.

It was the first time in my life you had trusted me with such a task. Though I read everything I could, I'd lost my nerve for sharing anything with you since you ridiculed my enthusiasm for Ian McEwan when I was a teenager. This was my chance to prove myself. I was anxious, forming wild fantasies of your amazement at my literary nous. So I brought you some books – not the books I had found myself, not the writers I was really into, like Lydia Davis or Ali Smith, authors who, I realised after you died and I was no longer afraid of you, might have been catalysts for change in your snobbery – but a pile of the books I was reading for my MA. I'd only begun a couple of months before, so it was a reading list for early Modernism. *Death in Venice*, plus *The Immoralist*, *The Outsider*, *The Unnamable*. I might as well have paid a literary consultant for a list of books to torture a dying late-twentieth-century poet. You read some of *Death in Venice* and then abandoned it by the foot of your bed, a reminder of my unwitting cruelty, and now here we were in the bothy with nothing to talk about. Whether or not that was on your mind I'll never know, but in any case we couldn't talk about books.

On the other hand, I had essays due and I was worried about them. You got ill just before my course started, so I hadn't been an entirely focused student. I knew you loved explaining things to me so enlisting your help seemed like a good ruse. As soon as I mentioned the essays, your face brightened and you asked me to show you the titles. I brought them up on my laptop and started to read them to you but you shook your head, took the laptop off me and stared at the screen to see for yourself. I chewed my lip, waiting, wondering what you would say.

But after an extended period of frowning you handed the laptop back and said, 'Those are unreadable to me. Those sentences don't make sense.'

I stared at the questions myself, feeling better and

worse than I had before. Better because you didn't understand either, you whose head to me seemed bigger than the British Library. If you didn't understand, nobody could. But also worse because, actually, if I read the questions a few times, they did make sense to me. Even if I didn't know how to answer, I could work out what they were asking.

You continued to frown at the screen over my shoulder until your eyes found Deleuze's name in the final question and you snorted. 'I tried to read him once in a hotel room in Paris and threw the book across the room in disgust,' you said. 'It made no sense. It was a load of rubbish.'

I put my laptop down and picked up my whisky while you stared more fixedly at the TV. I could make no more sense of the programme we were watching than you could make of my essay titles. I sat there wishing for a cigarette, listening to your lungs, knowing you were listening to them too, feeling certain I wasn't the only one of us thinking we should never have come.

You gulped your whisky and tapped the empty glass against my full one. They were small glasses ridged in an intricate pattern along the cup with sturdy necks like vases. To your delight, I'd found them in one of the cupboards. You had the shorter glass with the bigger cup. I had the taller more fragile glass with the emblem of a cricket club on the side. The whisky was a pale orange colour and burned my throat. It tasted like woodchip and petrol.

'It's all right,' you said, 'not the best stuff, not single malt.'

You made a face like an apology, as though I really was a young friend you'd invited round for this disappointing whisky. Your wife had chosen it, you said. There was a helplessness about the way you accepted the things she'd bought for you, as though it was entirely beyond you to have chosen yourself. It was in the same helpless tone that you asked me, 'So what are you going to do while we're here?'

'Apart from work,' I said, 'I guess I'll go out for a walk.'

That was when we hatched a plan we could both get excited about – I would walk into town and buy you some single malt whisky. I looked on my phone to see where the nearest town was and found it was four miles away. A three-hour round trip. Both of us seemed happy with that. Three more days together in this small place was beginning to look unbearable. I'd walk to the nearest town and buy you some single malt whisky. You thought that was a brilliant idea.

Then we turned back to the TV. It occurred to me that this was what I'd always wanted – the chance to be bored with you, the chance to watch rubbish TV with you, the chance to sit on a sofa not talking to you. I'd spent my life coveting dads who were domestic, dads who were annoying, dads who wanted you to do your homework and go to bed so they could watch some history programme you ridiculed them for. Now here you were, my very own at-home dad, sitting next to me, doing nothing, your face slack and your eyes on the screen, your lips as good at finding the whisky as the tiny, striped, pixellated figures were at wrestling each other for the cone-shaped ball.

When the match ended, you said you'd go to bed. 'It's the driving,' you said. 'And these drugs she gives me. I'm tired. I get very tired.'

'It's okay,' I said. 'I'm sleepy too.'

I wasn't sleepy, but I was relieved. You weren't as drunk as I'd seen you but I was glad you wouldn't drink any more. I helped you stand up off the sofa and I held your arm to walk you to the bathroom where you brushed your teeth and pissed while I paced the corridor, waiting to walk you to bed.

'So strong,' you said again.

I thought, Yes, that's what I'll be for you – a daughter who doesn't baulk. Who can walk an eight-mile round trip for a bottle of whisky, who can lock the door and not worry about strange noises in a lone cottage in the middle of nowhere with no one to talk to late at night.

We said goodnight, see you in the morning, and you shut the door and I thought that was it. But a few minutes later you started to cough. Your cough shuddered through the house.

I ran back, shouted, 'Daddy?', opened the door.

You were sitting up in bed, collapsed forward over your knees, coughing and coughing, your tongue out, face turning red. You were holding your nebuliser and I went over and put my arm around you.

'Daddy? It's okay. Are you all right?'

'I need that morphine.'

I ran back to the kitchen and looked in the medicine bag and found the bottle. I brought it back. You unscrewed the lid and took a swig. You stopped coughing. You put the lid back on, tried to screw it and couldn't, handed it to me, your eyes down, bloodshot. A second later you looked up, grinning.

That grin. That big froggy smile. Something in it made me feel like your conspirator, as though there was an understanding between us that I wouldn't make a fuss, that I would let your pain be yours alone. That was the defence mechanism between us, wasn't it? The one you'd developed, which I'd inherited. Share something painful or hurtful, say something blunt and real and almost unbearable, and then put that grin on your face. I smiled back with the same glee.

'It sometimes happens with my little Rain Cloud,' you said. 'But we mustn't blame it, it means well.'

You stroked the tip of the nebuliser that was still puffing out milky smoke.

Your Rain Cloud.

It was supposed to help you breathe, supposed to do something to your lungs to loosen all the phlegm and whatever else was down there that you kept coughing up. You said it helped. All I saw was that it made you cough. You called it your Rain Cloud because when it was first delivered by the nurse, and she showed you how to hold it in your mouth, how it let out steam in these pretty white swirls, the thing that came to your mind was an obscure, antiquated love poem about a man who misses his lover and asks a rain cloud to get a message to her.

Your Rain Cloud.

It was the kind of thing everybody loved you for. The feats you made turning something distressing, or uncomfortable, or seemingly quotidian into delight, into poetry. I took the Rain Cloud from you and screwed the lid tight on the morphine, passed you a glass of water and gave you a hug. 'I love you,' I said and you said, 'Goodnight.' Then I took the morphine and the nebuliser and went out and shut the door. All along the corridor I could still hear you breathing.

In the kitchen I boiled the kettle, found a clean pan and took apart the Rain Cloud, placed it inside. Your wife had shown me how to sterilise it. She was retired but worked on Wednesdays, so I had been going round then to look after you, since you'd had radiotherapy and couldn't be left alone. I liked those Wednesdays. The biggest challenge was getting you to eat. I always stopped off at the shop on the way and bought anything I could think of to entice you – salted cashews, prawn crackers, fancy honey to have in Lapsang Souchong tea, Magnum ice creams, crusty bread and good butter to make

Marmite on toast instead of the margarine you always had in your fridge. I'd brought some of these things with me, and ate a spoonful of honey while I waited for the kettle to boil.

I was also waiting to hear from my boyfriend. I'd texted him earlier but he hadn't replied. We'd been arguing recently and as I ate the honey, I went over some of the things we'd said. It was easier than listening to you breathing. The kettle boiled and I poured it over your Rain Cloud, thinking of all the germs obliterated in an instant. It calmed me, this small cleaning ritual. I put the kettle down and stirred the parts with a fork. Then I found my phone – no messages, but I set a timer. Five minutes soaking time.

I went to turn on the TV and decided not to. I tried to write another message to my boyfriend and rang him instead. He didn't answer, but a minute later he rang back. It was Friday, he'd been at work, he was on his way out again now. We chatted for a few minutes about his work and where he was going.

Then he asked, 'So are you having fun with your dad?'

'Sort of,' I said. 'It's kind of weird being here.'

He said nothing, but I heard him swallow his breath. When the silence had grown uncomfortable, he said, 'Well, is the place nice?'

'It's all right. There are hunting pictures on every wall.'

We breathed down the phone at each other a few

minutes longer and then he said he had to go. 'I'll ring you tomorrow,' he said.

'Okay.'

Embarrassed by my sadness and inability to speak, I shut my phone in the kitchen drawer. I decided to make a slice of toast but got impatient and ate warm bread instead, spooning bright red jam on to it. Since you had been ill I had started to be afraid of food again, or afraid of myself around food. I could not trust the urgency of my hunger in this long, empty night. I finished it in three bites and then washed my hands, went to see which books you'd brought with you.

Your bag was still on the table, unzipped, the books stacked inside it. The stack was in fact all one book – you'd brought two dozen copies of the same book with you. Your book. It was your poetry collection that had been published earlier that year. *A Monastery of Light*. A beautifully designed hardback in blue with a white shape like a tombstone on the front and on the inlay page a photo of one corner and window of the house in Greece. The tombstone shape was in fact the shape of the house's windows, the similarity a coincidence nobody noticed until it was published. The poems inside were all about Greece. They were also all about death. They were my favourite among everything you'd written, and you'd sent the manuscript to me as your first reader six years before. The poems had been written, you told me, just after I left, the Easter I visited you out there. That trip was the only other time

I had stayed alone in a house with you. I'm in one of the poems, the first one.

> Death is an acrobat performing in the skies. He
>   doesn't need a net. He's dead already, yet,
>   he somersaults on stilts before our very eyes.
> The sun is a day-torch blotting out the stars. What
>   is it looking for in this world of ours?
> Death is the answer. When the sun sets, taking
>   death with it, the stars appear to contemplate
>   deathlessness.
> Death is the answer. I look in the garden where
>   my sweetheart used to play, now a pigsty with
>   the droppings of a donkey on my way.
> Death is the answer. The roof has new tiles. The
>   balcony is new. The workmen on their ladders
>   are hammering it to you: the former occupants
>   are dead and you will be so too.
> Death is the answer. Death is in the tears falling
>   down my face when my daughter appears.
> Standing in the morning, she asks, looking all
>   around, Daddy, will this house last forever?

I remember the moment you're writing about and I remember the tears that are in every line of that first section. It was the same trip you told me about the washing-up. Perhaps this was the morning after. I remember asking you that question, working up to the moment. I had wanted to ask you that question all my life. It sounds like the question of a child, and several people reading the poem, figuring out it was me, have believed until I corrected them that I was there with you as a child, asking it. But I was nineteen. Too old, perhaps, for a question like that, but I had wanted to ask you as long as I could remember. I had been worrying about it. Would it last forever? What could we do to make sure it did? How could we hold on to the things that had happened there? How could we keep it alive?

To see that you'd packed twenty or so copies of your own book made me laugh. That was good. It loosened the atmosphere. I loved you for what you were. Crazy old poet, crazy old narcissist, serious man with your serious tasks, serious about things I loved too. The timer went off. I poured out the water. I laid the pieces on a tea towel to dry and upturned the pan in the rack. I made a mint tea and sat on the sofa to write my journal.

I had been thinking about the myth of Narcissus because we had read some of T. S. Eliot's *The Wasteland* on my course and it had brought to mind the idea that myths and their meanings could be other than those I'd been taught. Narcissus is a proud young man known for his beauty. Echo falls in love with him but he rejects her and is cursed by Nemesis, the goddess of revenge. One day, walking in the forest, he catches sight of his reflection in a pool and falls in love with it. Unable to leave his beloved, Narcissus remains by his reflection in the pool until he dies. Echo stays with him, her own life fading to nothing. Beside the pool where he died, flowers grow – narcissus flowers, their bright heads bent as though staring at themselves.

My mother had always called you a narcissist and my brother took up the word also. Any time I was upset with you – because you'd said something hurtful, forgotten to call, cancelled a visit – that was my mother's retort: 'Xanthi, he's a narcissist. He is completely narcissistic.'

Or as my brother liked to frame it: 'Xanthi, I don't know why you're still doing this. It's like you're talking to the cat and getting upset, going, "Why won't she talk? Why won't she talk? I keep talking to her and all she says is meow."'

I had adopted the term myself, though it troubled me to apply it to you. And yet that evening, sitting up alone in the bothy while you coughed yourself to sleep in the other room, I realised that I hadn't understood the word at all. I hadn't comprehended the scale of it. It wasn't that you thought only of yourself but that your reflection was the only bearable image, the only place where the fragments of you fitted together as one whole thing. The image was too precarious to withstand any ripples in the water. If I wanted to be close to you I would have to stand at your shoulder and look.

*

In the morning I got out of bed before you, though you were already awake. I could hear you breathing. All night I'd woken up to the sound of your coffin.

Coughing.

All night I'd woken up to the sound of your *coughing*. I wrote the wrong word.

I wrote the wrong word and scared myself. But it's true. I couldn't sleep all night because of the sound of your coffin. With every noise, all night, it hovered closer and closer.

This lack of sleep made me feel strung out and I splashed my face with cold water before I went in to say good morning. You said you'd like some breakfast so I brought you cornflakes in a bowl with milk. And coffee. Instant, two teaspoons of it, added the water, then a glug of evaporated milk until it turned the colour of cut pine. I made myself a strong black tea and sat cross-legged on your bed watching you eat. We both liked the morning. I liked the crunch of you chewing, the splash of your spoon in milk, the simplicity of giving this to you. We talked about the owl you heard outside in the night, the invisible distances a person travels in sleep, what films we might watch later. I'd bought you *Forrest Gump* on DVD after your hip replacement the summer before, when I found out you hadn't seen it. You'd been waiting since to watch it with me.

'We can watch it this evening, I promise,' I said.

'It's important,' you said. 'It's my medicine. Like these cornflakes. They do much more good than the drugs.'

Yes, and for me too, I thought.

You got out of bed and got yourself dressed and took your first drugs of the day while I made myself a green smoothie and put on some music.

'What is that slime you're drinking?' you said when you came into the room, but you didn't hear my explanation.

I was about to repeat myself, thinking it was some pain inside you taking your attention but I noticed your expression was benign, curious. You didn't look at me but I watched you sit down on the sofa, frowning as though at something beyond the walls. You didn't speak until the song ended.

'This album you've put on,' you said.

'It's *Street Legal*,' I said.

'I know that,' you said. 'It reminds me of your mother.'

I didn't say anything. I watched you being reminded. I listened to Bob Dylan growl and saw my mother, the two of you, decades ago.

You kept on with that faraway face for another song. Then you said, 'She is just as beautiful now as she was thirty years ago.' You said it with certainty, an irrefutable fact. A kind of marvelling.

I watched you turn this knowledge over and considered all the things you'd said about her that I could not fit together. It brought out in me a special kind of love for you when you said lovely things about her. I stood behind the kitchen counter drinking my green slime and wondering about it.

Then the moment was too much and you sat up, losing your faraway look, and said you were amazed 'that machine' – my laptop – could play music. We'd tried and failed to get the stereo in the place to work last night.

'The speakers aren't very good,' I said.

'No, but the songs are all there.'

Then because I asked, teasing you a little bit, you explained why you'd brought so many copies of your book. You had a job to do, you said. Your main task of the weekend. You had to sign and number fifty of them, and also choose some quotes for some special edition copies of your new collection *The Land of Gold*. These would be in hardback with marbled covers, signed, a handwritten quote on a plate on the inside cover. Your task was to choose twenty-five different lines to write on small pieces of special paper that were to be fixed into the books. You had to look through the collection and choose the lines. You said I could look over the shortlist later, help you choose. Then you sent me away.

'You will have to be in a parallel world,' you said.

I went to work in my room for a bit. I was working on a novel, a second draft, changing bits, adding bits, trying to work out the structure and the narrative arcs of each character. It wasn't going well. After an hour or so I gave up and packed a rucksack to walk to the town. I packed a bottle of water, some pens, a notebook, my phone and purse and put my shoes on. I interrupted you to say I was leaving.

'It's called Sissinghurst,' I said, 'that's the nearest town.'

'That's where Vita Sackville-West used to live,' you said. 'The great love and muse of Virginia Woolf. See if you can find some evidence of them.' Then you wished me luck and I left.

Four miles, mostly on B roads. Country lanes with no footpaths. I was walking in the long grass, the ditches, getting stung by nettles, trying not to get run over. The soles of my shoes were loose and the mud sucked at them. I was convinced I would get lost. My phone was old and didn't always work and the app I had for maps was outdated. The blue dot that was supposed to show where I was kept jumping around and there was no way of looking at what shops there might be in the town. It was the end of 2013 but I was years behind with technology. I'd been wary of it, but now I felt stubborn, foolish. At the same time it was a relief to be out of the house and to fill my lungs with the cold, leafy air.

I made it to Sissinghurst in an hour and a half and found a shop. It was the one off-licence in the town. I asked for a bottle of single malt whisky. The proprietress asked for ID. I didn't have any. I explained the situation. I had come to buy whisky for my dad. We were staying nearby. It was a present. I left out the part where you were dying of cancer. A man came into the shop and she asked, 'What do you think, is this girl over eighteen?'

He looked me up and down and said yes.

'All right,' she said. 'That's thirty-six ninety-nine.'

I had the money. Two rolled-up twenties you'd given me for the purpose. I'd told you I didn't need it but you insisted. The truth was, I did need it, and I could tell the woman thought so too. The long muddy walk hadn't done any favours to my scraggly hair and clothes.

'I guess it's not so usual for a young woman to come into your shop in the middle of a Saturday afternoon and buy an expensive bottle of whisky,' I said.

'No it is not,' the proprietress replied, but the man disagreed, and everybody laughed, and I felt like I'd passed, for the moment, as a regular kind of person.

She wrapped the bottle in rough creamy paper and I put it in my rucksack and thanked her and left. The door closed with a jangle and I felt the heavy bottle tip, the liquid swishing at my back. The high street was sparse and flat, the shop fronts plainer than I'd imagined after you'd told me who had lived there. I walked up and down looking for a cafe to get a hot drink before I started back. The place I found was full of groups of women in nice clothes, families with large portions of cake and scones and bubbling conversation. I was conscious of my old coat, dirty boots, the high probability I carried that smell of you with me. But the waitress gave me a table in the corner and brought me an expensive tea in an ornate pot and I absorbed myself in making spider-diagrams for the characters in my novel. It would never have mattered to you, I thought, if everybody in the place thought you were mad.

An hour passed, then another half, and I felt more like I was on holiday. I realised that I was on holiday, in fact. That a holiday was what this was supposed to be – or 'a retreat', as your wife called it. But holidays had not been holidays this year and every day off work took me closer to not being able to pay my rent. I had taken on several extra students this term to try to pay off my overdraft. It had been a bad summer for work. The summer was always difficult for finding tutoring work, and after you'd got your diagnosis I hadn't tried hard enough to find any. So I drank my expensive tea and let myself forget everything else, staring at the page with all those conversations rising up and fading out around me. I was about to ask for another tea when I looked at my watch and saw it was past three o'clock.

Three o'clock, with an hour and a half to get home. But it got dark just after four.

I got up and bothered the waiter by paying at the till, felt his eyes on the bottle of whisky when I put my rucksack on the counter to dig out my purse, gave more than I could afford as a tip in my anxiety and hurried out, walking halfway up the high street before I remembered it was the other direction.

What if you'd tried to call when I had no signal? What if you couldn't get to your phone fast enough? What if you were scared and there was no one there with you?

I'd been gone almost four hours. I cursed myself, thinking how obvious it was, my wanting to get away from you. I scrambled the same paths going back, tripped in brambles, cut my hands grabbing branches when I had no time to find my balance. I kept checking my phone to see if you had rung, staring at the bars showing how much signal I had, certain they were lying to me. Besides, your phone was unreliable, and if you started to die wouldn't you call your wife?

I made it back in three-quarters of the time, reached Split Tree Lane before the dusk had set and thought I must be in the wrong place because it hadn't taken long enough. But there was the bothy, that long narrow house like an abandoned section of freight. The curtains were drawn, I wasn't sure if the lights were on. I ran the last few steps to the door, tugging the handle so hard I couldn't open it. Then it swung at me, twisting my arm, and I flung myself inside, yanked my shoes off, feeling the badness in me slipping into everything.

There you were, sitting on the sofa watching TV.

I said, 'Daddy, have you been all right?'

You said it had been a historic day for Australia in the rugby, though Scotland had put up a good fight.

I took a chair at the table facing you and saw that you'd spread your things out over it. There were two stacks of your books and your heavy fountain pen between them, a scalpel beside the can of SprayMount. Underneath was a single sheet of lined paper, covered in your handwriting, scratchier than usual.

'I've got a lot more to do tomorrow,' you said. 'Then I'll need to borrow your mind for a few minutes.'

'Choosing the quotes?'

You nodded, vaguely, and towards the screen, your hands clasped over your lap. I watched you and then couldn't stand the silence between us, the rugby commentary, the way your handwriting didn't look like it should.

'I got the whisky,' I said.

I brought the bottle over and you changed your glasses to see it. You had one hand on the bottle and the other on my wrist and when you found the words 'single malt' you pulled me in for an embrace. I couldn't keep my balance, one shin diagonal across the cushions, and I fell forward, winding myself trying not to crush you. I heaved myself back, kneeling beside you. You held the bottle up to the light to show me the colour before putting it down on the table.

'You're an angel,' you said.

I told you the ID story and you laughed.

'Twenty-five years old!' you said. 'I was serving beers in the Colony Room aged five and a half.' It was the small-town mentality, you said. You were surprised they'd stocked such a fine bottle of whisky.

You wanted me to get the glasses straight away, but I said there were goats and chickens just outside the door, they'd come to visit, so you agreed to come and see them first. You put on the shoes I'd insisted you bring with you and we walked a few steps around the garden. We watched the chickens and goats scratching in the dead leaves, the grass and dirt, their eyes flashing in the dull light. We talked about the ways they moved, their small noises, gentleness. Then you said you were cold, and there was fear in your voice and that fear went straight into me. We hurried back inside. I helped you back on to the sofa.

The rugby highlights were playing and I watched them with you, hypnotised by the commentary I didn't understand, the precision of the players' movements in slow motion. You told me some stories about when you played it, stories I'd heard dozens of times before, but I listened and questioned you anyway. And it was good to hear you tell again your favourite story, how you were the captain of the English Schoolboys, a team that was completely undefeated for several seasons, how their record still stood today. Then you told me also the closing story of your rugby days, how you couldn't stand the drinking and the gang mentality and resigned from the team and your teammates were outraged and hunted you down that night during a drinking session and beat you up. I'd heard this conclusion several times before but that did nothing to change how your expression, your voice, the hurt you still felt troubled me. Then it was whisky time.

Six o'clock, whisky time.

The way you checked your watch.

The way you said the words.

The way you looked at me out of the corner of your eye.

The way you expected me to clear the table, bring the glasses, hand you the bottle, demanded snacks.

Not like I was your daughter-servant, more like I was your trainee accomplice. There was an old-fashioned mischief to it that for a moment made it impossible, or irrelevant, that you were ill.

We were two men again, I thought, eating salted peanuts, drinking whisky, all our feelings only shadows in the room.

'Yes this,' you said, raising your first glass of the new bottle, 'is how it should be.' Like liquid sunlight, you said.

We watched *The X Factor* and I tried to learn your enthusiasm for it, tried not to look at my phone so I wouldn't be disappointed my boyfriend hadn't rung. Your wife called three times, and each time your voice became softer, your responses flimsier. The third call, she asked what we'd had for dinner. You'd muted the television so I could hear her surprise that we hadn't eaten yet.

'Xanthi,' you said after you'd hung up. 'You've forgotten about supper.'

You were scolding me, but you had a big grin on your face and toasted me with your third glass of whisky when I suggested sausages and mash. I refilled the bowl of nuts, calculating how long it would take to cook, if I should sneak away the bottle of whisky.

We ate at the table and you teased me for the minimal amount I'd put on my own plate – a spoon of mashed potato and peas – saying women had such strict rules about what they would eat. It occurred to me then that you'd forgotten about the time, three years earlier, that I tried to tell you about my trouble with food. I thought perhaps I could say anything, tell you anything, and you would set in your mind only what you wanted to hear. You'd asked for a bottle of wine with the meal and when you'd finished you left your plate and carried it and your glass back to the sofa. I did the washing-up and watched you take careful sips, your hand steady and your eyes on the TV. By the time I'd put everything away and come to sit with you, it felt like too much time had passed for us to talk again.

Then you found a programme about space.

You loved space, the night sky, stars, galaxies, the expanse of it, the impossibility of knowing. When we sat up late outside in Greece you would point out the constellations to us, explaining how they moved as the planet turned. You said it gave you comfort. Watching this programme with you I felt comforted too, as though looking at outer space our bodies did not matter at all, nor the ways in which they let us down. Then they showed a close-up of a dust particle. A grain of space dust magnified so that it looked as complex as a living organism.

'You know what dust is?' you said.

'No?'

'A non-entity, but it begins absolutely everything.'

'It's beautiful.'

'Well, exactly.'

'Like in your poem, isn't it?'

'Yes,' you said. 'The *mu mesons*. Particles so small they can pass through the Earth without noticing it's there.'

I remembered your wonder when you first explained them to me, the focus in your eyes as if trying to see them passing through us as we sat there. The way you had of allowing me in for a moment, so the two of us saw the same scale expanding the world until all its gaps were visible. We watched the grain of dust as it rotated, quivering on a background of black. I could not think how my life would be without someone in it who said things like that.

When the space programme ended, you said you were going to bed. It was just after nine o'clock. I helped you down the corridor to the bathroom, brought your medicines and the Rain Cloud, waited to take it away and clean it again.

Alone in the kitchen, I checked my phone. There was a message from my boyfriend, sent an hour ago. It said he'd been at the cinema and was heading home. He'd ring me when he got there. I called him, but after a few rings the line went dead. I tried again but there was no answer. A few minutes later he sent another message to say he was talking to his housemates, if it was too late he'd ring me tomorrow. I dropped the phone and then picked it up, turned it to silent and shoved it between the cushions on the sofa. Then I stared at the blank TV for a long time. Then I stared at the hunting pictures on the walls.

You weren't asleep. I knew because I could hear you coughing through the walls. I bit my nails and picked at the loose cuff on my jeans.

What would I do if you stopped breathing?

Give you morphine for the pain, that's what the doctor told you – if it happens, take morphine, don't stop. Your oxygen tank, your Rain Cloud.

What if I needed to do CPR?

What if I needed to call an ambulance?

What if I had no signal?

What would I do first, call an ambulance or tell you I loved you and didn't want you to die?

And under all this, the feeling that you were ashamed in front of me. You weren't the mystic poet embracing death after all. It was winter and cold and wet and dark and you were dying. And there I was, still scrabbling at you for some feeling, some reason I was certain I needed when you had nothing left to give. And there you were, coughing yourself to sleep while I stared at the walls and ran out of nails to bite and dug my teeth into my lips instead, trying to drown the feelings in the iron taste of blood.

*

The next morning, Sunday morning, was easier. This was our final day. Your wife was coming to pick us up first thing on Monday. I brought you cornflakes and coffee on a tray again and we talked about the women kept in domestic servitude because further details had been on the news and you kept saying 'anathema' and I didn't know what it meant and you explained it to me.

'It means the very thing that is repellent to you, that cancels you out. A curse – the divine curse on a person that casts them out of the Church, in fact.'

Anathema. What a word to be given. The thing that feels as though it will crush you. And a tangible thing for you to give me, proof that there was more to come between us. For years afterwards, I use the word whenever I can. That man is anathema to me. That way of living is anathema to her. Toast without Marmite was anathema to my dad. I use it for effect, misuse it, throw it in when nobody's expecting it. And every time I do I am sitting there again at the end of your bed with the clean pressed white sheets in the bothy in the room that for those few moments was full of something other than your death.

You still had work to do, you said – photographs of your book launch to stick in your journal, quotes to choose. You told me again I'd have to be in a parallel world. So I worked in the other room, kept the music off to hear any emergency, stared at the screen of my laptop and could not remember what I'd meant by anything I'd written. Around eleven, I sent a message to my boyfriend to ask if he'd be around tomorrow evening when I got back. Then I had to hide my phone again because I was afraid he wouldn't reply.

We had lunch – cheese and pickle sandwiches, at your request – and afterwards, you asked if I'd brought my drawing things.

'Of course,' I said. 'You asked me to, so I brought them.'

'Well it's not always like that.'

No, I thought, not everybody in your life has been so hell-bent on pleasing you.

I'd started drawing a couple of years ago, doodling with black fine-liners, mostly animals covered in abstract patterns. It was a way out of anxiety, a displacement activity. But you liked them. You were outlandish in your praise, called them 'genius' and 'remarkable'. You said I could make a lot of money. Your praise embarrassed me, partly because they weren't that good, and partly because it was in contrast to the way you spoke about my writing. I wanted you to speak like that about my stories, and the fact that you didn't and that you were so insistent about my talent for drawing gave me the suspicion that you thought I was a bad writer and were trying to save me from a life of failure by coaxing me on to a different artistic path. It was a constant doubt, a nagging question. I had written and published one story that you liked, but since then anything I showed you received little more than an awkward nod and a change of subject.

But my drawings – you had a lot to say about them. You wanted me to draw you a coelacanth.

'You've got a job to do,' you said. 'I've commissioned you.'

There was a coelacanth in one of your poems, that's how we'd first begun talking about it. You loved the story of that eighty-million-year-old fish, thought extinct since records began, only to be discovered in hoards at the bottom of the Indian Ocean by some fishermen in the 1960s. I loved the story too – the giant fish's indifference to its own non-existence, the insouciant eye I imagined it cast on the passing boats. I loved that you loved it and that you understood that I understood why you loved it and loved it for the same reason. We shared a penchant for mystifying true stories, an eyebrow cocked to facts, an eye-roll at the suggestion of impossibility, as well as admiration for the unlikeliness of the coelacanth's design: its solidity, its ugliness, its mammalian limbs, the way it hadn't changed in eighty million years.

I said I didn't want to get it wrong, I needed an image to draw from.

'You can look it up on that machine,' you said.

I googled it and showed you the page of images and you pointed to one and said, 'Yes, that's it,' as though the others were different fish altogether.

Then I set to work. A piece of paper, a row of pens, a pencil for the first sketch.

'You must have music while you're drawing,' you said.

I put on Townes van Zandt, one of the compilations I'd made you, and you sat on the sofa to listen. They were songs you'd heard for the first time a year ago but already knew every word to. An hour passed like this. I didn't notice you get up or come back, I didn't notice you breathing. When I had finished I rubbed out the pencil lines and took it over to show you.

'Here, Daddy.'

'What is that?'

The way you said it – 'What – is – that?' Emphasis on every word. You said, 'That is just incredible.' You said, 'This morning it didn't exist, and now it does.'

2.

One of my favourite memories of you, perhaps my favourite memory of you from the time you were ill, and perhaps of all the time I knew you as an adult (I think if I listed my top fifty memories of you, the first forty-five would be from before I was thirteen), is the late afternoon of Sunday 21st July 2013, when I came to see you after I'd got back from your brother's seventieth birthday party.

There are always moments between people who have ongoing, shifting relationships that are more or less intimate, more or less satisfying, more or less treasured, and it's never clear to me why this should be, why there should be moments with a person when whatever alchemy you are to each other doesn't take, has no effect. And yet sometimes it really does exactly what it is supposed to. This is one afternoon like that, when whatever connection was possible between you and me came to life, walked around the room in front of us.

It had been a big party and I was hung-over, twenty-four hours of intense emotional experiences shuddering through me. I'd met relatives I'd never spoken to before, everybody had asked about you – and I rang you on the drive back to London to tell you I was too tired to come. I'd been visiting you often since your diagnosis three weeks before, possibly too often, and sometimes felt that it annoyed you. You were captive, bedridden on one lung, had not expected the summer to go this way. It was the most social you'd been in my lifetime. You kept saying you had work to do, you couldn't keep wasting all this time with visitors. So I didn't expect you'd mind if I rang up to say I couldn't make it.

But you were crestfallen. You said if I was tired I should take a taxi, or your wife could pick me up. You said I must come, you needed to see me.

I said, 'Okay, of course I will,' and watched my mum roll her eyes in the rear-view mirror.

You'd never spoken to me like that before. I was moved. I ran all the way down your street in my impatience. Your wife answered the door. She led me upstairs to your room and, unusually, didn't come in.

'Xanthi.'

Your voice. Your face. The late-afternoon sunlight through the Velux windows over your bed. Your clean shirt. Your tan skin. Your combed hair. Your wrists like tree trunks, shirt sleeves rolled up, legs tucked under the coarse beige blanket, a small stack of books on the wooden chair beside your bed. The clay letters of the words 'Holy Spirit' lined up on the shelf by the wall beside you: clay letters in pale blue, yellow and white that I made you as a child, that had been there ever since. The light in that room. The way you said my name. The way you looked at me when I looked at you.

'You made it.'

'Of course, Daddy.' I hugged you.

Your shoulders like the boughs of a tree. The solidity of you, the particular smell, your good smell, the right one. Silver chain at your neck, ichthus hanging over your T-shirt under your unbuttoned shirt.

Nothing had started yet. There had been no treatment.

You were just a man whose lung had collapsed, who'd been told he had a tumour the size of a tennis ball growing where his heart bordered his left lung. You were just a man who'd been told there was no cure, that this was almost certainly what you would die from. A man with daughters, son, wife, siblings, friends all wanting to see you.

There was talk of steroids, antibiotics, morphine, oxygen, but none of this had happened yet, nor the commode chair, wheelchair, crate of Ensure. What someone had given you: a crate of wine. Australian wine from your Australian friend. 'Green wine', you called it. That's what you offered me today.

I sat cross-legged on your bed like always. Other people could pull up a chair, but I liked to sit that way, liked to pretend I was at a party with you, that we were two young people at a party with not enough chairs, having a conversation we had years to return to. This sitting on beds with you was a new thing. Since I was a teenager, we'd met in cafes, on park benches, in your car. When I was little there was no time to sit down: we had work to do, building rabbit hutches, stalking dinosaurs in the Natural History Museum.

Somehow, sitting on your bed you looked like you were on holiday, a sunbather on a giant recliner, the sea breeze coming through your Velux. It was a hot summer, mid-twenties and higher, there'd been no rain or wind for weeks. You asked me about your brother's party and I told you. I felt guilty for having been there while you were in bed, for spending time with the family you were now almost estranged from, for wanting to go even though you couldn't. I told you the booze ran out and you said your brother should've known better, that your mother would've been dismayed. It was a version of you I liked – one who pre-dated me, who cared about other people and social occasions. It was a point of honour, for you, how brilliant your mother was at hosting, though I had never seen you host anything but that one disastrous dinner where the guests left early, offended.

'Let's have some green wine,' you said. You told me to go downstairs and get a bottle.

I was worried that you shouldn't be drinking, but you scoffed and I felt stupid. What else were you supposed to do? Though you did concede it might be a good idea to get some snacks too.

Green wine. I've been looking for it since. It wasn't officially green. It was white wine, but with a green tinge.

In the sun it looked green. In your hand it looked green. In your eye it had magical properties. I have tried to work out what it was. There is a Portuguese wine that translates as 'green wine', made from early grapes, white grapes with the skins still on. That's not it. There are other wines whose names approximate 'green'. There are white wines that look close to green in the right light, but I can't make myself believe it. Or maybe it's that I can't make my eyes do what yours did. Like a toy an adult has made talk that goes limp in the hands of a child.

Green wine, balmy sunlight, the evening coming in. My hangover discarded, exhaustion driven away. You had all these things you wanted to talk about, racing through topics with an energy I hadn't seen in you in years. But there was one thing in particular you wanted to tell me. After you'd had your first glass and I'd poured you another, you took my wrist with your free hand and pulled me towards you.

Smiling, your face close to mine, you said, 'Three months.'

I said, 'What?'

'Three months,' you said, 'that's what they gave me.'

It took me a moment to understand what you meant. 'Three months?'

'Three months.'

I did the calculation and immediately felt ashamed, my maths brain drawing your death nearer.

3rd October.

I saw it already as a certain fact, like someone holding scissors up to the year.

You were watching me. That look in your eye like a knowing elder, someone who does not believe the younger generation will think him credible, but who holds on to the truth anyway. You said you hadn't told anyone else, nobody knew but the two of us.

I asked, 'Who told you, when did you hear that?'

You said that you had known from the beginning, from the first day, when you went in to get the prognosis with my sister and your wife. You said at the end the others walked out and you held the doctor back, a young woman doctor. 'Very beautiful and very intelligent,' you said. You held her back and asked her, in cases like this, how long do you think? You said she answered you plainly, she understood you wanted to know and that you wanted to know only for yourself. Three months, she said. She told you three months. You said you understood then how it was.

Three months.

And you looked so fucking happy about it.

Like someone had given you the key to unlock the meaning of your whole life.

I loved you in that moment in a way that shattered so much of the version of you I had built up over the years, that felt like proof of its inadequacy, of its meanness. I loved you with such a force too in that moment that I could forgive myself for the bad thoughts I'd had about you, and see that you trusted me, knew what I did with the things you told me.

Three months.

We sat there thinking it. Then you started singing that song.

I'd never heard it before, so your tunelessness meant nothing – it was the lyrics that struck me: you were going to see a spirit of the sky, you sang, it was where people went when they died. You smiled vaguely as you sang, your hands dancing.

I stared at you. 'What's that?'

You sang some more. 'It's a song, an old pop song. I've had it in my head for weeks. "Spirit of the Sky", by Norman something, I don't remember.'

I repeated his name, repeated the name of the song. You nodded and I took out my phone. I typed in the song name, the name Norman.

'Norman Greenbaum, "Spirit *in* the Sky"?'

'Yes, that's it, how did you know that?'

I pressed play, waited for it to load, then turned the screen around.

Your face.

Your eyes.

Your face like a little boy's.

Your eyes like a teenage boy's.

Your whole body leaning forward in delight.

In black and white, a man with long dark hair, a long-sleeved, loose, seventies shirt, handlebar moustache, blank expression. He looked stoned, spaced-out, a face of the seventies that was disconcerting today. The clapping steady rhythm, the swing of it, the clanging crescendo, the backing singers, the lyrics.

Fucking hell, I thought. Are you serious?

The song you'd had in your head was this wailing hippy guy singing about dying as though it was a very exciting show he'd been invited to?

And yet I understood straight away it was a song you would love. Something shining in it. A crystal clarity. A pop song, yes, but with words like lyric poetry. A jauntiness to it, the electric guitar, the fact that it's someone young singing it, the Christianity. It was a celebration of death, both reverent and irreverent. You used to dance to it, you said. You loved the wizardry of my being able to conjure it up on my phone, that there he was, Norman Greenbaum, swinging his wrists and drawling along to that song you hadn't heard in decades.

I played that song at your funeral.

When I play it now, years later, you're still there, sitting with me on your bed in the yellow sunlight drinking green wine, staring at me like I have done something miraculous, and letting me know it's okay you're going to die.

When someone is given a terminal prognosis, the future disappears. There are no days you can plan for, the calendar looks evil. You think something simple like,

I wonder what we'll do for my mum's birthday next week? and your gut uppercuts your lungs and you can't see anything but funerals, tears, panic, death. You know it will happen, but you don't know when, and so every day declares itself as death day. You are living in a state of emergency. You are braced for death.

I had panic attacks throughout your illness, though when they started to become regular, and thoughtless, when they started to appear in circumstances that apparently had nothing to do with you, I stopped connecting them to you. I thought I was just losing my mind, or that this was just how I was, a panic-stricken person. It could happen anywhere. I would lock myself in the toilet at bars, sit down on the pavement on the way to the supermarket. I went to sleep and woke up through every night and in the morning convinced this would be the day you would die. I guess that's what my brother and sisters and mother and your wife were avoiding when they refused to believe it was terminal. They didn't want to live in a state of emergency. Or perhaps they did and I didn't know about it. I don't think anybody really knew how anybody else felt.

There were all these things I wanted that I thought I would get. I thought it was a necessary condition of the end of your life that there would be certain words exchanged, certain resolutions made. I hated myself for this disingenuousness, for all this wanting, and for how hard it was to hide my anxiety. I thought something would happen, or there would be some conclusion. I thought you would say sorry.

We sat listening to that song and then you wanted more wine, more music. I remember you holding my hand. I remember how the translucent greeny-yellow spilled out into the room so it was like we were contained in the liquid we were drinking.

I remember that you wouldn't let me leave. I thought it was time to go, perhaps – we weren't saying anything – and you said, 'Not yet, please don't go.'

I got another bottle of wine. You asked me to put on Townes van Zandt. We sat there in the green winey sunlight, breathing together, and I was aware of how close I felt to you, how much of your sadness was seeping into me, and how sad it was to sit with you. How it was something of the particular thing between us, to listen to these songs and not speak. I felt like a young man with an old man, not your daughter but the student you'd nurtured from adolescence. There was nothing of the child wanting her father, nothing of the abandoned baby, none of the hurt.

And then the CD ended or the wine ended or the light changed or the moment just exhausted itself, and it was me and you again, and still you wouldn't let me leave.

I made a joke about it, a joke to cover my hurt. I said, 'Daddy, it's funny, sometimes I'm not allowed to see you and now you won't let me leave.'

You said, 'What do you mean, not allowed?'

I said, 'Sometimes when I ring up, your wife says you've had too many visitors today, you're too tired, or there's someone else there, I have to try another time.'

You frowned. You shook your head. You made the face I liked you to make, your protective father face. You said, 'No, that's not right. That's not right at all. You must come whenever you like.' Then you took my hand. 'You're my special one.'

Did you really say that? Was my heart big enough to take it in?

Did you say that to all of us?

I stayed with you until it was late, until it was dark. We talked about things that usually bored you – the children I was tutoring, my house, my friends. You wanted me to stay with you. For once you wanted me to do the talking and you listened and thought about whatever I had to say. The balance of power had tipped in my favour. It was getting close to the time you usually went to bed, but still you wanted me to stay.

When I finally said goodbye you hugged me and let go then hugged me again, and only agreed to my leaving because I told you my boyfriend was cooking for me. You waved me off, sitting in your bed full of this terrible joy, and I waved and told you I loved you several more times than I needed to.

That night is like a cup of your liquid sunlight in my memory. I can feel you, hear you, see you tipping your glass of green wine, smell it even. It is like an anaesthetic. And do you know, Daddy, what I found this morning, in a small notebook, handwritten? The name of the wine. Toolangi. I googled it. Toolangi wine. It's from a vineyard on the edge of the Yarra Valley in Victoria. I am going to track some down and drink it by your grave one bright afternoon very soon.

It is an anaesthetic, and that's why I'm remembering it now. Because I need something to get me through this Sunday night, the final night of our trip to the bothy. Though I would like to, I can't leave you there, in July, forever. I have to go back to November, where everything is different. There is no more sunlight, no more green wine, no more singing along to long-forgotten pop songs from the seventies. Seven weeks have passed since the deadline of your life and you have a piece of mesh holding open your left lung, the tumour still broadening in your chest.

I had just finished drawing the coelacanth. You named him Cyril and propped him up against your whisky, which, I noticed, you had started to drink. It was four o'clock. The sun was disappearing. You hadn't yet turned the TV on.

I don't want to remember what happens next. I don't want to remember the rest of it. I don't want to follow the story to the end, turn the mess of memory into words, a story.

I am twenty-nine years old. Four years and nine months

have passed since then. I am not the daughter any more who spent those four days with you in that cottage in Kent. You are no longer the dad who sat beside me on the sofa with nothing to say, with everything inside you I was determined for you to tell me. That tension is gone. No matter what I write or remember or reimagine, there won't be a different outcome. There has never been anybody I wanted to talk to about what happened after you died as much as I wanted to talk to you. You know the answers, the secrets. I am free now to show anybody the inside of my head. I can't hurt you any more, and I know also that it would have been impossible to hurt you then. That my love for you has infinite dimensions, and more space in it than I could have imagined, space enough for fury, bitterness, childishness, resentment, your wife, my mother, my brother, my sisters, all the old men you found so much more interesting than me, all the young women. I was fighting for scraps of you, not understanding that a person is made of multitudes, is made of dark matter, is made of the silent voice of DNA that goes on forever, tangling through flesh and sperm and egg cells across generations. You are here now as much as you ever were. You are the air and the table and the loose screws in the shelf in my room that you made and the fact I think writing this is worth doing at all.

Daddy, Daddy, Daddy, do you remember?

You fell in love with Catherine Zeta Jones in *Entrapment*. I made you dinner and sat beside you while you watched it, the coelacanth looking back at us. We drank more wine and whisky and I thought I could forgive your love for her, pressed up close as you were against a great, blank future stretching out. I fetched my phone, finally, from the pile of socks in my room. There was a message from my boyfriend saying he was busy the following evening, but suggesting Wednesday or Thursday, possibly, for us to meet. I replied to say either would be fine, trying to ignore the creeping feeling in my belly. It seemed obvious to me then that the relationship would soon be over. I tried to think how I could save it, what I could say to stave off his rejection, the inevitable loneliness. I bit my nails, read his message again. But when I looked at your face, still watching the television, I felt a tinge of gladness to know there were still things that might not outlive you.

Bored now of the film, you flicked through the channels, settling on a Hitler documentary. We watched a bit and then you started coughing, really coughing, and I became afraid. I put my hand on your back, suggested morphine, water, counting breaths. When you stopped I went to hug you and you shrugged me away.

You said, 'I'm terrified of being asphyxiated.'

'Are you okay? You're okay. Do you need to sit up?' I was fumbling for words that would soothe you, put walls and floors and ceilings back where they were supposed to be.

Then you settled again and we chatted, your eyes on

the TV and mine on you. I was trying to get the conversation to a place where I could tell you how I was feeling.

I thought, It's the last night, this is my last chance.

I wanted to tell you how much I would miss you. But I was clumsy, embarrassed by the glib fact of my health, my strength, my future. I said something clichéd like, 'You must know how much everybody cares about you.'

What you said next made me chew blood from my cheeks in the effort not to cry. 'It's impossible to know anybody. What does it mean, to know someone? The more you love someone, the harder it is to know them. Look at your brother: sometimes he is so sweet and gentle and then other times he's not there at all.'

'What about your wife?' I said. I was fumbling. How could you believe this? I wanted you to change your mind.

'I know her less than I know anyone.'

That took my skin off. The way your eyes seemed to ask the air in front of you. You didn't look at me, just drank your wine.

I felt your truth seep into me, how it made a shambles of reality. I told myself, No, for you it is impossible, for you maybe, but it's not impossible for everybody. We *can* know other people. We do know them. It's only for you that they're mirages. I was teasing out your logic, using the old tools of my philosophy degree.

I thought, If you want to be pedantic, fine. It is impossible to have a subjective sense of what it's like to be another person, but in the everyday sense of course we can know people, it's what we all depend on. I couldn't bring myself to argue out loud, the words froze on my tongue.

And you kept shaking your head, believing it. You were insistent.

You started to cough and I tried to give you water, reached out a hand to rub your back and didn't touch you, said I could get the morphine and you batted me away. Bored of it, that's how you looked.

You said, 'How can it sneak up on you like that? I had no idea.'

'It's really hard,' I said.

'No the thing is, it's lung cancer, it keeps changing.'

'There are so many parts,' I said.

'To be confronted with your own mortality, that's terrible, but then the small things take over.'

The small things.

I sat there with my legs curled underneath me on the other side of the sofa and wanted to say I understood, but knew that would've been ridiculous. I didn't understand what you were facing at all, and at that moment I felt that I was nobody to you. Here we were, at the end of everything, you were finally broken enough to tell me how you felt, and I had nothing for you, could make no sense of it at all. It was the first time I'd appreciated how little you wanted to die.

You said, 'Cancer sucks the life right out of you. You're all flimsy and deflated.'

You said it in a way that reminded me you were a man, and once a young one – an athlete, a carpenter, one who could drag a tree down a mountain on his hip – still a young man, perhaps, inside. A man who didn't want to be flimsy and deflated. Just because I saw you as so old and decrepit, it didn't mean you saw yourself that way. Or maybe it was being so close up to death that made you realise you wanted to live.

I said, 'You've been so brave, so positive.'

You said, 'I have to be and I'll continue to be.'

I said, 'You can be sad, it's okay to be sad.'

I was thinking how someone had said that to me, and I said it because I wanted to give you something, but hearing it I understood that the same words addressed to you were absurd. Sad about losing your own life? There could be no more licence to feeling.

Things had started to tip. Your patience was running out. Everything I said was making it worse and you were looking at me like I was a stranger.

I said, 'I was all over the place, I was a mess, but then I'd see you—'

'You're twenty-five now, you can take care of all that yourself.' You growled it.

I understood that was all you could stand of my feelings and I swallowed them, put them away. Your eyes were wet and alien and narrow. I realised two-thirds of the bottle of wine was gone. The second bottle. I'd barely touched my first glass.

'Maybe you shouldn't drink any more,' I said.

'No, I'm not going to,' you said, finishing your glass and pouring another.

You sank deeper into the sofa. Then you started to cough again, worse than before, it overtook you. Your whole body convulsed. I took the glass from you and placed it on the table, knelt on the cushion beside you and stroked your shoulder, the feeling of your bones so close under your shirt making me afraid. Your coughing slowed and you nodded at me and I sat back. Our hearts were racing. We were both getting hot. There wasn't enough air in the room.

You tossed your hand at the TV. I thought you were going to say we should stop talking and watch it but you said, 'This is making me paranoid.'

It was still on the Hitler documentary. Black and white footage of Berlin in the thirties, propaganda material. There was a desperate edge to your voice, an abrupt horror, like something in the documentary was climbing into you, that hell beckoning – your fascist-state cough – and I had not protected you, would let the evil of the world eat you alive. I tried to find the control, almost fell off the sofa looking for it, hearing your horror voice over and over.

I found it. Changed the channel. Morecambe and Wise, another documentary. The story of their rise to fame. You settled, you smiled, you told me something you remembered about them. We watched for a few minutes. I considered taking away the wine. But you weren't necking it any more, just taking occasional small sips. I tried to concentrate on the show, thinking that I didn't know anything about these comedians who clearly meant something to you. But then a new section started, after Morecambe had a baby. Family life had begun. There was discussion of how this affected their work.

You were appalled. You tossed your hand at the TV, glugged your wine. 'It's so *weird*,' you said.

'What is?' I said. 'Being a comedian?'

'Domestic duties are not compatible with creativity.' You burned with the phrase. I realised you were talking about Morecambe's baby.

The great weirdness of life was Morecambe's baby. You were afraid for your life but angry still that someone could prove you wrong. And I still had it in me to resent you for it, to fester with my silent retorts. To pity you. Because if domestic duties were compatible with crea-tivity, then why had you sacrificed them your whole life?

All night you kept repeating, 'You see I'm not hiding anything, I don't want to hide anything from you, I don't want to be that kind of daddy.'

That lightness, teasing, soft tone mixed with your fear, surprise at every new pain in your body. You'd go from this levity to melancholy, laughter to fright.

You said, 'I don't know what's going to happen. It could happen here.'

It took a moment for me to understand what you meant and then you started to cough and couldn't stop.

Your face was strained. 'I need to get to bed,' you said.

I was stuck watching, moments behind. You couldn't get up off the sofa. You fell back on to it. Fell again before I could move and stood to heave you up. You were lighter than you'd been but your legs weren't working. You had no balance. I heaved you up and you put your arm around me, gripping me by the ribs. We shuffled down the corridor to your room. I was afraid every moment I would drop you, afraid you would start coughing and I wouldn't be able to hold you up. The corridor was so long, your bed so far, the hall so dark with no lights on. My ribs hurt, arm hurt, heart hurt.

Why had I let you drink so much? Did I want you to die?

There was no one to ask, no one to ring, no one to make decisions for me. I could feel myself spinning into the pitch dark outside, looking for someone, anyone, or just a place to hide among the goats and chickens.

We made it. I helped you into bed. I helped you out of your shirt. I asked several times if you needed to wee. You wanted morphine and I fed it to you on a spoon and you were calmer then, stroked my hand, my arm. The covers were pulled over your legs and you were hunched forward, not sleeping yet, but your face was relaxed. The panic was over. Mine as well as yours. I wanted to cry and I wanted to sit there, watching you, all night.

But you were calmer then. Calmer than I was. Perhaps it was the morphine. I looked at you. I tried to breathe normally. You were still trying to breathe at all.

You said, 'Who knew there could be a daughter like you?' Your voice was hoarse, slight, a wry gasping.

'What do you mean?'

'I appreciate your caution . . . your intelligence . . . your wisdom.' Your voice shuddering, strained yet precise, a voice I didn't know.

I looked at you, your head still bowed, your eyes still focused down at your chest. I said, 'I love you, Daddy, I love you, you're a . . . dad, well.'

I didn't know what to say you were. I didn't know what you were. I was frozen with emotion and relief. I put a glass of water beside your bed, a box of tissues. I told you they were there. I told you to call me any time during the night. I said I was right there, anything you needed at all. I asked you again if you needed to wee.

You said, 'God bless.'

I turned out the light. I went back to the living room. My hands were shaking. I was certain your wife wouldn't have let you drink so much. I was scared you'd vomit, choke on your own vomit. I was afraid you would wet the bed. But more than any of that I was afraid that in the morning I would find you dead. And yet all the time the words you'd said to me went round and round my head.

Caution, intelligence, wisdom.

You really did love me, then.

I told myself you'd passed out drunk a million times, that you wouldn't vomit, that you'd been drunker. My hair and clothes were saturated with you.

I didn't ring my boyfriend and he didn't ring me. I didn't read anything. I didn't watch TV. I wrote in my journal and then I sat staring into space while the gaps between your bouts of coughing got longer, and when I hadn't heard a sound from you in a quarter of an hour, I got up and went to listen at your door. I listened to you breathing. I wondered about you, the nights you'd spent like this, all that wine and whisky, the strength of your stomach, liver, bladder, the state of your heart, the state of your feelings when you woke up in your clothes. Did you remember? How much did you forget? You weren't strong enough any more to be showered and combed and have breakfast ready before your children woke up. You weren't strong enough to pretend your need for alcohol was anything to do with poetry. You weren't strong enough to walk down the hall on your own. But you were still alive, asleep, full of your own thoughts and ideas, conflicts and urgencies and angers and resentments and reactions, full of all your own pain, and still strange to me.

I got into bed, everything that had happened circling inside my head, all your different faces and words and expressions, the versions of you, and how they had all kept rising up in you, overtaking your single body on the sofa. I had been nobody, I thought, all that evening. I had been not a person but a witness. And yet you had taken my hand and sat up for that small moment and said those words to me that made me feel seen.

Did Narcissus ever turn around to Echo and say, I needed you?

It was hard for you to need anyone. We were there, all of us, but you didn't know how to say, 'Come in.' You didn't think it was possible to know us, and so you didn't try.

Is that true?

Sometimes I think everything I write about you is a lie, and you are laughing at me, quite kindly, a conjurer setting me quests still, trying to stretch my mind from wherever you've got to. I don't know if you are my dad any more or if I have become you; if the you I am addressing is no longer a separate person, but has become something in me. If I have dived into the pool and am swimming in the dappled fragments of your reflection. I have seen those yellow flowers and they are beautiful.

I must have slept, eventually. The next morning your wife arrived to drive us home.

"Coelacanth"

xrb. The Bothy 24th November 2013

The carpenter

At the end of 2013 you went to Wales with your wife. It was a trip you made every year, staying in the rural north for a month over the holidays. The doctor said there was no reason for you not to go this time, as long as you took your medications – you had no further appointments booked and there would be a hospital nearby.

I could see several reasons and petitioned you with some, though I was afraid of sounding harsh or selfish, of telling you what to do. You were still alive, after all, had recovered somewhat since the radiotherapy, yet the future was murky. Everything felt mixed up: it was hard to tell what was hope, what was medical euphemism, what was delusion. All I knew was that I felt sick at the thought of you going. You didn't seem too sure yourself, but nor did you seem equipped with the clarity of mind needed to make a decision.

In any case, the week before Christmas, you left. I was certain you wouldn't come back.

At home over Christmas my mum and brother took turns reassuring me, though I doubted their confidence since they had seen you less than I had, knew less of the minimal facts the doctors had been able to share. The alarm I felt at not seeing you for so long at this critical time took my breath away. Everything was short-circuiting inside me. I did not know what to do from moment to moment, how to get from one end of the day to another.

Perhaps you picked up on some of this, or perhaps you felt something like it yourself, because on the phone the day before you left you suggested I come out and see you for a night when you were there. I wavered. I couldn't be sure how serious you were, how your wife would feel about it. Our trip to the bothy was also on my mind. Apart from that, last-minute trains were expensive and the journey would take a day each way. These things might have been trivial but for the fact I had very little money and a 6,000-word essay to write. I'd tried to defer the course a few months ago but was told I'd have to pay for the whole year again. It had taken me years to save up the fee. Continuing seemed like the only thing to do.

When I told my mum and brother what you had suggested, my brother laughed, but my mum winced and I thought she looked almost afraid.

A few days after Christmas you asked again if I would come and I had to tell you it wasn't possible. I hated the sound of my voice saying it, the sound of your 'Okay', the taste of something like prescience, that I was losing my last chance to see you alive.

I kept telling myself it wouldn't happen, that death in your case was unlikely to be sudden, while my essay was due on 2nd January. So I lay on the floor of my old bedroom at my mum's flat, reading *The Sound and the*

Fury to find examples of alienation. The story had begun to make sense at last – too much sense, possibly. I kept reading and rereading the section I had chosen where the character gets ready to die until I didn't know if I was reading or hallucinating. When it came to writing anything down, I couldn't formulate a single thought. Even the length of a sentence, I realised, was enough time for you to die. I would start to type and my ears would invent a phone ringing so I had to jump up and check. At times I was afraid to breathe or move, as though if I didn't I might stall time, save a few moments of you.

In the end I did get a call, but not the one I expected. You were coming home early. It was too cold out there, you said, and the house where you were staying had too many stairs. I started to ask if you hadn't checked that it was wheelchair accessible before you left, when I realised what you were saying.

What you weren't saying.

I swallowed, trying to both hold on to and escape the feeling that was in your voice. 'When?' I said.

You told me the day after tomorrow. Would I come and see you the day after that?

We agreed a time and I hung up and felt everything inside me collapse, like whatever awkward pain had been holding me up for two weeks had been dismantled. And yet I continued to stare at the blank phone screen, trying to work something out. Something different about our conversation. There had been no mystery in

your voice, I realised, no particular charm, no special-
ness. It was a bald, dull, tired request. Then I went back
to staring at the cursor flashing on my bright white
laptop screen, telling myself over and over you would
survive until then.

Somehow time passed. My essay began and then it was
finished. I went to New Cross to hand it in, managed not
to cry with frustration over the library printers, took
the train home again, slept. Then it was the day and I
was on my bike, so full of words and feelings my mind
had glazed over. I might have been swimming through
the wet, fume-filled air.

You answered the door in your slippers and one of
your old jumpers that had gotten much too big. You
looked shabby and shuffly and a little bit distracted but
as I wheeled my bike into the hallway it occurred to me
I couldn't remember the last time you had looked so
alive. Though your wife had bought you new clothes
better suited to your slenderness, their smartness
troubled me far more than your familiar outsized ones.
This was a jumper I knew you in, no matter the loose
threads or how it drooped almost to your knees. You
folded me in a half-hug and led me to the front room to
sit down. Upstairs was too far, you said, with a backwards
wave of your hand.

Your wife said she still had unpacking to do so I made
us tea and asked about your trip. You answered vaguely,
brushing me off – yes the mountains, yes the trees, no

the journey was all right – but not without adding at the end, in the same tone, that perhaps I had been right, it wasn't where you wanted to be. I couldn't look at you then, could not bear to acknowledge it, though a wave of nausea went through me.

I told you I'd finished my essay but didn't think it was any good. You said you'd like to read it and I shrugged. 'I'm not even sure what I wrote,' I said.

We talked like this, quietly, simply, and every now and then you coughed so hard I thought I could hear your insides clattering against each other. Then you would hold a handkerchief to your face and spit into it, collecting whatever came up. Each time, afterwards, you frowned and tucked it away again, an inconvenience now more than anything, while I tried not to imagine what parts of yourself were decaying in your pocket.

Then our conversation petered out and you stood up. I thought you were going to dismiss me. I froze, ready to protest, when you asked if I'd got my shoes on. But you said, 'I've got something to give you.'

You opened the back door, waving me away when I offered to get your coat, and stepped into the damp dregs of the January day. I followed you across the mossy brick patio to the sheds you'd built against next door's extension wall. You opened the door and pointed me inside.

'That box,' you said, 'you'll have to carry it for me.'

I lifted it.

'And that bag,' you said. 'They're too heavy for me now.'
I took that too.

'Are you all right?'

I nodded, not wanting to show I didn't find them heavy at all.

Inside, you told me to put both on the table and gestured for me to sit down again. With no further explanation you began taking out one item at a time and holding it up to show me. 'What's that?' you said.

'A coping saw.'

'What's that?'

'A hacksaw.'

'What's that?'

I laughed this time. 'A hammer.'

You pointed to the other side, raising your eyebrows a little.

'That bit's the claw.'

You went on until I had named everything. Then you pulled the plastic bag towards you and pulled out your drill. It confused me, that it should be in a plastic bag. It seemed so unlike you to take so little care over where it was stored. I wondered when you had last used it, where it had been. Then I remembered you had brought it to my house in Whitechapel when I first moved there to fix the bookcase you'd built me to the wall. But that was almost a year ago. I tried to find the plastic bag in my memory of that day – it was thick, green, a silver logo almost rubbed out – but when it appeared there I could not trust it. I remembered holding up the book-case while you cursed and sweated, gritting your teeth to press the drill through brick. I had thought then that if you couldn't do it, nobody could, that I had never seen you defeated by any task or object. And you did it. The shelves had stayed there for twelve months. They might have remained there still, but I was moving again and the bookcase would come with me. Except this time, I'd have to tackle the wall myself. The flat I was moving to was at the top of three flights of concrete stairs.

I didn't know how much of any of this was on your mind. Before Christmas, you had told me it was your one wish to see me in my new home, and I had humoured you, said yes of course you would come, not knowing when care tipped over into cruelty in the field of expecta-tions. In any case, you didn't mention it this evening. I thought again of your voice on the phone. In that same voice, you asked me to plug the drill in, and then you pressed the button to show me it was working. Its buzzing growl filled the room and I noticed you smile – the tip of a smile only, a slight narrowing of your gaze. After showing me the two settings, you placed it down.

'It was my father's,' you said, 'now it's yours. I have no use for it any more.'

Before I could respond you held up two bits, asking if I could see the difference.

I nodded.

'Do you remember what they're for?'

I told you.

You nodded and put them back in the box. Then you slid the box and the bag over to me. 'Well,' you said, 'that's it. Take whatever you can fit on your bicycle and you can pick the rest up later. Share them with your brother, all right?' Then you sipped your tea that must have gone cold by then, replaced the cup and pressed your palms down against your knees, looking up, as though ready for the next thing.

But we both knew there wasn't any next thing. How could there be, when there was so little of you left? Your body inside your clothes was the only material proof; if I took the tools from you there would be even less. I understood something had happened but I didn't know what – if it was the trip, the new year, some new symptom, or time itself. If it was only the quiet that came before the end. Whatever it was, I wanted to hold on to it, to stay there drinking tea while the night came in, sitting in your creaky wooden chairs with this last piece of you. I didn't want to take your tools because I didn't want to think of you not having them. But the way you said it, I had the idea you needed me to take them. That you wanted to give me one last thing. That this was and wasn't the reason you'd called me over as soon as you'd got back.

'Thank you,' I said.

*

Less than an hour later you watched as I strapped everything to the back of my bike with bungee cords, insisting to your wife I would have no problem balancing. She had lent me a larger bag to keep everything dry – the early evening had turned the damp to drizzle. Then you waved me off and shut the door and I tried to concentrate on the road, the traffic, the route to my new home, not what it meant to leave you there, all your tools clanging in a Bag for Life behind me.

SSB's Dictionary

Numinosity: an inner glow. The quality of a work that makes it art. The sign that a work is complete, that it has come to life. E.g. 'That story is a living breathing thing – it has numinosity.'

Temporary

You died and the house didn't. That was always going to happen.

You died and I learned the Greek for 'died' and 'cancer' and 'sad' and 'wanted to be here' and 'January' and 'lung' and in the end did not use any of it. When I told your old friends you'd died, there were no questions, only clasped hands and nodding heads. It was expected. Four people had died in the village that year. There were more empty houses than inhabited ones. Many had been inherited from grandparents by young families who returned from Athens only for the warmest months, leaving after the August holiday. Inhabited houses were neighboured by ruins, roofs falling in and cacti sprouting through glassless windows and rotted doors. And then there was the engineer – his wife had left him and his heart disease was getting worse. He'd been told to stop drinking but instead he'd started drinking from sunrise to whenever he lost consciousness. When I told him you'd died, he shrugged and turned away from me, back to his *tsipouro*, suddenly engrossed in something on the floor.

I had taken my sadness to the place I thought it would make most sense, and instead all sense had been flattened.

The house didn't care about any of that. It didn't care

you'd died. It was still there, the same as it ever was, dying at a rate we could keep up with.

It was there that spring when I brought the news – the walls still a metre thick, the trellis still painted yellow, the door still arched, opening with the sticky sound a honey jar makes. The balcony, your copper jug, your wooden plates, your shorts still in the trunk, your T-shirts, two gallon bottles of wine waiting to be drunk. The bills had been placed on the table by the cafe owner, the address two words only: your first name and the name of the village.

I was there with my boyfriend and didn't want to be. I made this obvious, watching myself as though in third person giving one-word answers or drifting into the kind of deep, focused remembering that appears catatonic from the outside. I watched him tread on the dusty floorboards and wanted to explain to him who had laid them, how you'd rubbed beeswax into them, that the table was made from the offcuts, why there was a trap door over there. But I couldn't rouse in him anything more than friendly interest and soon this in itself infuriated me, as though it proved the house didn't warrant anything else.

What more did I want? I wanted you.

You had not outlived our relationship, as I had hoped. I would have swapped him for you in an instant. I had no ability to modulate my feelings, everything roared through me and he bore the brunt. Perhaps I wanted him to leave me, so that I could be as desolated as I felt. It was only three months since you'd died. I didn't know three months could be described as 'only' then. On the last day he and I walked on the beach north of the river – that broad, sparse stretch of sand where once we were attacked by a swarm of biting flies and fled to eat our lunch in the Lada, do you remember? – and I started crying and couldn't stop, and could not speak to explain it, and lay face down in the sand until my eyes were full of grit and told him to go, to leave me here, I was never going to get up.

When we left the house at the end of the week, I thought I would never go back.

But six months later, the craving came back. The smell of thyme, bright hot sunlight, the thought of the scar-legged cat and her kittens who lived feral on the mountain – glances of memory coaxing me. My mum and brother were going in the autumn and I bought a ticket to go with them. The bleakness I felt at the beginning of the year had undergone a centripetal inversion that summer and by August I was elated. Everything amazed me.

Back at the house, I felt like you were there with us, you'd sunk into the walls and we were staying inside you. I spoke to you every morning, drinking coffee watching the sun light up the mountain, tipping your cup at the psychotherapy tree. It was completely different to my previous trip. My mum and brother knew the name of that tree, that it had been rescued from growing under a rock and with a little psychotherapy survived, only with a kink in the trunk. They understood the importance of the fig tree growing through the cement steps. They knew the significance of the stone slabs placed as four seats behind the house, no matter how overgrown with thorny branches. They did not baulk at the shower soaking the entire downstairs. The inhabitants of your stories, we were back, just a little older, to argue over the different versions, a plurality that you would never allow.

I found a bedraggled jumper of yours in one of the trunks and wore it every evening when the sun disappeared into the valley and the house took on a chill and the three of us ate dinner at the table made of floorboards, listening to rembetiko and drinking tea or water from your copper jugs. We had come home to you. We slept and ate and talked in your walls, a hint of you in every cup of coffee or glance through the window. At least that was how I felt. Between the three of us, we spoke little of you. Our pains clashed. Often it felt as though we were grieving different people. Besides, it was obvious to me then that you hadn't died, but only side-stepped into another form, one that could finally match your hugeness.

I thought you had escaped death, but in the end it was more like the other way around. Your death had escaped me. I'd missed it, somehow. After three years I had accepted that you would stay that way – dead and not dead, hovering around, whispering to me forever. But in October 2017 we went back again and you were gone.

*

I knew it as soon as we arrived.

Nothing had changed – the roof was still crumbling, woodworm still lay curled on the floor, the bills on the table still had your name – and yet there was a difference. Something perceptible. The house was only a house – the house our dad built. You were there, but you weren't talking. You weren't there watching. You were there only because you had been there, a memory proved by what you'd made.

You weren't there. You were something to be missed.

I'd looked for it, that difference, for so long. So it wasn't a sad thing, or not only that, but something good too. Because I could finally feel it, your absence, and a small part of the pain fell away.

When you died nothing in my life changed at all. Everything was exactly as it always had been, except for a missing name in my email inbox, one less letter on the doormat every couple of months, no old man standing at the door in his bird-watching coat, wanting to tell me about a poem he just wrote. Tiny details, hard to track in the complex soup of experience.

You took up such a small fraction of my life, what difference did it make if you disappeared altogether?

That was what had been so hard, to have to search so thoroughly to find some trace that you were gone. I couldn't hold on to it, the grief, and so I felt bleak and angry and outraged and then elated and free and monstrous. And I felt like a fraud whenever anyone showed me sympathy, or shared their own stories. I felt like I didn't miss you. What was the difference between an absent father and a dead one?

This, I thought, that October – this, this, this.

You were gone. This is what it felt like. You were gone and you weren't coming back.

The house was ours now. You weren't going to turn up and explain anything to us. If we didn't fix the roof, it would leak until it caved in. There was the difference, the crack – a small space for loss to sit down for a moment, let itself be known. We took the bills with your name on to the bank and paid them. I didn't bother this time to explain that you'd died – my Greek was never good enough anyway – just paid and smiled and left, let you live on in this bureaucratic way.

The drawers were still full of papers with your writing on them. They still are. Fragmentary notes or phone numbers or unplaceable names underlined. There are some damp, filmy papers with some of your poems about Greece scribbled on diagonally, as though you were catching the words incidentally, thoughts coming at you out of time, a side note from whatever you were doing. The cassettes are all yours – Mike Oldfield, T. S. Eliot reading his *Quartets*, bootlegs of rembetiko musicians your friends had recommended. If I wanted to live as you for a day or a week, I could do it there. Your books in the bookcase. Your shoes and T-shirts and jean shorts in the chest. Your toothbrush. Your pens and pencils and scalpel and funnels and the yellow boat you built so my brother and I could sail on the mouth of the river when we were babies.

I guess this is how many people feel when their close family members die and they have to sort through their possessions, a wasteland of symbols and memories. Except I wasn't used to it and so every single item felt remarkable. For years, I hadn't wanted a single thing thrown away, and any suggestion my mum or brother made of doing so invoked my outrage.

My brother wanted to buy a vacuum cleaner and get rid of the rat-chewed brooms. No, I insisted, I loved to sweep. My mum brought your dust-infested dressing gown from where it had hung for decades downstairs, holding it at arm's length, her face turned away. I took it from her and swore I would wash it, that it would be useful one day. Both had been trying to persuade me that we should buy a washing machine so we didn't have to wash all the towels and sheets by hand at the end of every trip. This appalled me the most of any suggestion. I *loved* doing the washing, I insisted, I'd do it all myself to prove it. I could see your face, laughing, at the same suggestion. You loved doing the washing yourself too. We argued, my mother, brother and I, every time we came here, and this October I was more vehement than ever. Even I could hear how unreasonable I was being, but that self-consciousness blurred my vision, made it harder to distinguish what was important. Perhaps, now

I felt certain you were gone, I was afraid I would give in.

I broke a cup – the cup I always drank from, the cup that had been your cup – and began making plans to glue it back together, searching the toolbox for superglue, when my mum said, 'You know almost everything here was only ever meant to be temporary? They were just things we picked up to use while the house was being finished. None of this was meant to last forever.'

She's wrong, I thought, she's just saying that.

I kept searching for the glue. Everything in the box was sticky, gritty, and the pieces of the cup crumbled more as I gripped them. I set the pieces down and real-ised it was cracked from three different points on the rim. I realised, too, that if I was honest with myself, I couldn't be certain it was your cup, or at least no more yours than any of the other cups. I couldn't be certain, in fact, that you had ever used it at all. It was just a cup. And when I found the glue – I was certain you would have the right glue – it was unusable, dry in the tube.

I was afraid to look too closely at anything in the house after that. I didn't want my mum to be right. Or, I didn't want her rightness to change how I felt. The gas cooker was attached by a rubber pipe which had been gnawed by rats and fixed with gaffer tape. The gas canister under-neath was a decade old and when it ran out the man we used to buy replacements off was dead and I didn't think anyone knew where else we'd get one. We had a small electric oven but that died. The telephone line had been gnawed through years before. The shower head was so blocked with limescale that the water sprayed out in agonising needles.

My mum kept buying new sheets and towels and my brother kept buying new plates and utensils and every time either of them had been there without me they had chucked some more things away.

It was hard not to appreciate a working toaster and kettle. It was hard not to appreciate how careful they'd been. They had taken note of the things that were special to me and saved them, despite their better judgement: the scratchy maroon towel and the chipped red metal table and the wooden bowls, split and furry with use. Here they were, my mother and brother, alive in the present, with all their understanding and gentleness, while I tried to burrow back into the past, as though it was a place I'd want to live.

Like everyone and everything else, you were only temporary, and that was fine.

And so at the end of the week, when I was standing knee-deep in sheets in the bath which was full of spiders and rubble and woodworm (dead and alive) and possibly scorpions, trying not to bang my head on the ceiling and cause more detritus to fall out – shreds of poetry magazines and cereal packets the rats had used to make a nest before we blocked all the holes to keep them out – and the skin of my legs was burning from the laundry powder and my hands were blistered from wringing out the towels, I thought, What point am I making?

Sometimes I think my mum and my brother used five times more towels and five times more sheets than they needed to just to show me how mad it was for me to be tramping in hot water in the dark inside while the sun glowed, when I didn't have to. We could buy a washing machine. We had the money now. We could put it downstairs next to the bath and it would be brilliant. The sheets would probably be much cleaner and no longer wake my brother in the night with his asthmatic wheeze. It wouldn't mean the house wasn't the one my dad built. It wouldn't mean anything, probably. It would become just another legend of the house – how you and then I used to wear your denim cut-offs and tread the filth out of the washing among the spiders in the bath. And like all the other legends, there would be the underside to it, the story floating around the story that did not belong in the legend.

The one that didn't feel heroic, or special at all.

Because no matter how enthusiastic I appeared about washing the sheets, I knew myself I was a fraud. There were some sheets I never got around to washing. There were some sheets that had been left for years. I found them that spring, three months after you died, and immediately bundled them back into the laundry basket. Every year they'd hiss at me every time I went downstairs and I'd pull them out, telling myself I would wash them this time, and discover again your blood. Your blood, from your toe, the last time you visited. You who insisted on doing the washing with your own feet ended up leaving with a foot that couldn't wash sheets, leaving sheets that couldn't be washed. I don't know what I expected: it was unlikely my foot-stamping washing would have been capable of removing the stains. The sheets had holes in anyway. They were decades old. I don't know if I wanted to honour you by washing them, or to keep them forever as proof you'd been alive. It was like that, in the early days, this new future full of unprecedented needs and wishes. How was I supposed to know what was worth what? In the end I let them live three years in the laundry basket, and then I threw them out.

That autumn in the house I dreamed of you every night, and in each dream you died, over and over again.

You were meant to pick me up at the train station, but you never came because you'd died.

You tried to bake a cake but the cake wasn't good enough and no one would eat it, so you died.

Your car broke down so we had to get out and push but we pushed too hard and you dropped off the cliff and were crushed and died.

My brother told me you were drowning, we set out to save you but got distracted on the way and took too long so you died.

I climbed all the way to the top of a fjord to find you, fighting vertigo and nausea, and met you there but when I hugged you, you went still and cold and died.

It was a cacophony of deaths, a fireworks display. You died and you died and you died.

Perhaps I needed that much evidence. You had been so abstract to me while you were alive – a possibility more than a breathing, moving person – that your literal death felt almost meaningless. I needed a version as evasive as you. Or maybe it just took me that long to let go.

It was the same autumn that I decided to let go of the ghost of my eating disorder too, the first time I let myself acknowledge that I still had a problem. I hadn't made myself sick in years, not since the boggling days of your illness, but had periodically decided to restrict what I was eating so that my weight dropped dramatically. I had begun to understand it wasn't eating or not eating that mattered, but the feelings behind it – what would happen if I didn't obey the obsession and stop eating, if I let whatever I was so afraid of show itself. For so long it had been food that was the problem, I didn't know that the difficult part would come later. It was the same with you – not your death that hurt, when it finally arrived, but finding a way to live without talking to you.

Sometimes I think I've found one, feel myself absolutely in a world without you. Other times it seems there will always be something in me determined to bring you back to life.

One night, while I'm writing this, I dream you've found the manuscript and written the whole thing out in longhand, comments and underlines all in your scratchy green pen. You're almost done, you say, without looking up, you'll get it back to me any minute. It's your indifference to either of our feelings that surprises me, the fact that what you're interested in is what I've made. I'd like to think that's how you would see it, that you wouldn't find yourself trapped inside any version but free to live among whatever emerged.

31st January 2018

Do you know I think for years I was hoping if I wrote enough about you, you would just stroll back into my life?

Every old man I saw. You had been dead so long and yet every old man I saw, I thought, Oh! there he is.

It just seemed so likely. You came back so many times.

Paul Auster spent his life looking for his dad who wasn't there. He says that even though his dad is dead, he feels like he has to go on searching. 'Death has not changed anything. The only difference is that now I have run out of time.'

We've run out of time, haven't we?

I was running so fast, trying to find you, I ran straight out of it. If I hadn't been so hell-bent trying to get you to tell me you were sorry, you loved me, you loved my mother, you loved my brother, it was okay, you might've been able to tell me some of the things I most need to know now.

I did it all wrong. I thought it was my death, not yours.

I thought it was the kind of end to a story that contains and expands the meaning of the whole. I thought life was a story. Or I thought your life was my story. But it wasn't. It was you on the floor wrapped in what I thought was a curtain, wondering how it came to be – had you gripped it and fallen? Could the paramedics find nothing else? – but later I understood it was your bedspread.

Your face looked beautiful, unconcerned. Your hands lay by your sides. I kissed you. My brother kissed you. I cried and did not know I was crying and knelt by your head and said aloud, 'We were supposed to have a meeting.'

I don't know why when we met you always called it 'a meeting'. I don't know why or how you came to say all of the things you said.

We were supposed to have a meeting. But we ran out of time, didn't we?

Like I thought we were on the same path, but we weren't. Now I have no way to reach you.

One week before you died, I sat beside you in your living room and said, 'Daddy, I don't know what I'll do when you're not here.' I was trying to be sincere, wanting you to say something that I could take out later, wear as a shield against grief.

You said, 'What you'll do? I don't know what I'll do! I'll be nowhere! How can I imagine being nowhere?'

I told that story so many times to different people and it always got a laugh. But it always hurt me somewhere secret, behind the ribcage, under the heart – to think of you nowhere. To think of you trying to think of yourself nowhere.

That same afternoon, you told me a story about some soldiers, the evening after their friend died. They got drunk and sang songs but one soldier remained solemn and silent in his room, appalled. That was, until the captain came and knocked on his door. He spoke harshly. He said, 'You think you're the only one grieving, but you're not. We're just as horrified and sad, but this is what we do. We have to be together.' And the solemn soldier realised he hadn't understood anything.

It wasn't until I was teaching GCSE English a year later that I realised you'd borrowed the story from *Journey's End*. You had slid the meaning around, too. The way you told it wasn't on the syllabus. The way you told it, it was about different kinds of grief.

'People show their feelings in remarkably different ways,' you said.

You looked at me then and I knew exactly what you were saying. I had not expected it, and I loved you for that.

Don't let anyone tell you you're not sad. Don't let anyone ask why you don't cry.

How did you know I wouldn't?

Not after that first hour, anyway – not at your funeral. How did you know so many people would comment on that? That I'd need the memory of your face, that afternoon, so I wouldn't start to doubt my own feelings.

But it's getting harder to remember. It's getting harder to imagine myself back there. I'm not the same at all any more as the little girl or young woman who was obsessed and entranced by you. For example, could I call anyone

Daddy? I can't imagine it. I can't imagine this person I am now alongside that other person I was before.

What do you reckon?

You know I loved saying that word as a child. It was so exciting to feel it coming out of my mouth and finding you there. I wanted to say it for fun. Make you look at me.

'Daddy?'

'Yes?'

'Um.'

It was always so hard to know what to say to you. And now I can say anything I want.

SSB's Dictionary

Flibbertigibbet: a frustratingly fickle person who says one thing and does another, changing their mind frequently with little conviction.

A good marriage is
paradise on Earth

One Sunday, four and a half years after you died, I lay on the grassy slope of Parliament Hill in the thirty-degree heat with a friend talking about our dead parents. We hadn't spent an afternoon alone together before. We hadn't talked about our dead parents before. Although I like to throw you into conversation at any opportunity, my friend doesn't do that with his mother. I knew only incidentally that she'd died. We were walking on the Heath and he was reminded of her and we began to have a conversation, a big conversation, and we lay down on our backs in the sun and didn't look at each other but stretched out and talked to the sky. We began by talking about the sameness in what we felt, the feeling of loss and the alienation afterwards, the long illnesses, the excoriating pain of wanting it to end.

Then I said how I felt surprised afterwards because I didn't feel this black orb of sadness swallowing everything, the feelings I had were more varied. I felt freed and baffled and furious, opened up to everything.

He said, 'I think I felt something closer to the black orb.' We considered this.

He told me what he thought it was like, this black orb – a cloak over everything, a complete lack of joy. He said it was as though a pillar of the world had been taken away.

I said yes, I agreed with the last bit, losing a parent meant some connecting factor wasn't there any more. He used the word 'rooted', and I thought of the image I'd got back then, of a swing with one of its ropes cut. But I felt guilty, as I always do, talking to people who have lost a close, parent-like parent, and jealous and naive – as although I could pass as knowing what it felt like, could join in conversations like this and write about it and get people with living parents to feel sorry for me, I didn't know really, didn't know the true extent of it, the raw cold pain of losing someone who you cared for so completely. That was part of my anger, at the time. Something I had to metabolise, to understand the dynamics of.

I remember talking to two other friends about it, who'd both lost attentive, loving fathers. Instead of feeling, as my brother suggested, that my pain was nothing close to theirs, I saw that my pain consisted of different parts. Several parts of the loss had already taken place before you died; your death was only the final fragment. Our loss, and the loss in situations like ours, was also made up of the events during your life, the months after you left, the years you spent away from us, the hurtful things you said, what this did to our mother. *And then* he died. That was the phrase I had in my head in the days and months afterwards, but I hadn't said it in years when I said it again to my friend on the Heath in the burning sunlight that was making us sweat.

'He left *and then* he died.'

The bastard.

I was trying to make my friend laugh, and I did, though as soon as I'd done so I regretted it. It wasn't funny, not at all, and it made me feel worse because I knew my friend never would or could have made such a joke about his mother.

My friend said he couldn't enjoy anything, could find nothing good at all in the world for months afterwards, for over a year. I didn't tell him then about the unexpected thing that happened to me the summer after you died, when I felt injected with a mesmeric joy and loved everybody and everything.

That summer, I stopped being able to sleep. I didn't need or want to sleep. The world felt to me extruded, brilliant, overwhelming, like I had become a caricature of the man you were sometimes, when you cried at starlight and school reports, wrote poetry about insignificant moments like sitting on a bench in the quicksilver sunlight. This feeling lasted from July until October, a kind of mania that took me through a break-up, a brief, excruciating new relationship, three jobs, the first draft of a novel, several gallons of alcohol and dozens of hours walking aimlessly around London. After that I was shattered and slept through most of the winter, waking up and going to work in a daze before worrying myself to sleep again. Your anniversary arrived at the end of January in time for my delayed devastation. I cried then, finally unable to deny that I'd lost you.

But even then the feeling didn't last but appeared and disappeared, arriving in tiny bursts punctuating your presence. I guessed there must be something wrong with me. Why couldn't I feel things in the moment they happened? It was the same charge my ex-boyfriend had made when we broke up earlier that month. Sadness at the ending and at the loss it entailed seemed so straightforward for him, while it brought out an overwhelming blankness in me. Or at least a kind of breathless scrambling that appeared blank from the outside.

This was my fourth break-up since you died, though only four and a half years had passed. I'd had more break-ups in that time than most people I knew had had relationships, and the obviousness of this fact was becoming harder to pin on circumstance. None of them had been easy and after each I was left with that bereft, washed-up feeling, like waking up because the covers have been pulled off. What I mean is, they weren't something I enjoyed. But I never wavered over them, never wondered about going back. Once something was over, I was gone.

There had not been any particular thing, any meanness or final act that ended our relationship. It was, in the words of my new ex-boyfriend, just another change of heart I had. We'd known each other before we were together so he knew my history, how many times I'd done this before. Still, he'd been surprised when it happened between us. So was I. I never meant to be the way I was.

Three weeks later, he wanted to meet up to talk it over and as I geared myself up to go, I realised I was rehearsing lines I'd said multiple times before. I was practising being a person I reserved for this purpose, a concoction of guilt, indifference and an evasive generosity. My main aim was to say whatever I could to cause the least pain in the least time possible. I had agreed to meet for his sake, I thought – if it had been up to me we'd never have spoken again. But I was getting tired of myself. This same thought had been troubling me for years: what if I was no better at sticking around than you were?

The evidence was mounting against me. For example, my boyfriend who had been there the year of your illness and death. The memory of that break-up still stung, years later. He'd been furious with me, and told me so, both of us hot with spat words over an uneaten dinner. How could I just leave all of it behind, he said, after we'd been through so much? He hadn't left me, he said, despite wanting to, through all my picked arguments and insatiable need for attention. Now I dropped him like it meant nothing to me. I tried to explain how I felt but, in truth, what he said made no sense to me. You had died only six months before. He felt entitled to his anger because he expected people not to just walk out of his life. He had no idea, I thought, what it felt like to lose someone.

But the disparity between us stayed with me after, amplified each time the situation was repeated. I wondered if there was something in me that wanted to hurt people as I had been hurt. I wondered if there was something in me that wanted leaving to mean nothing, so I wouldn't have to feel my own pain. I wondered if I would ever be able to stay with anyone, to maintain the enthusiasm with which these relationships usually began. But it wasn't so clear cut. Things came unstuck as I thought about them. What if the problem wasn't my ability to commit, but the fact I kept getting into relationships that were never going to last? The reason I ended that relationship was because I didn't like myself when I was with him. Tense with anxiety from the outset, assuming he would lose interest at any moment, I had tried my best to be the girlfriend I imagined he wanted. Until I didn't. And then I left.

What was that?

It was you, I thought. That's exactly how I used to be with you.

And it was happening all over again. There I was, in 2018, having the same conversations. But we were older, me and my new ex-boyfriend, and we understood each other better, I think. We sat side by side on his balcony, sharing cigarettes and sipping whisky, watching the traffic on the roundabout below. We'd been sharp with each other earlier. I said I found it hard to remember who I was when I was with him and he told me not to think so deeply about things, that I should try harder to 'muddle through'. I said it was him saying things like that which made me want to end things. Neither of us had expected this to happen. But we were drunker now, gentler, knowing there would be no other time, that this would be our last conversation.

He said, 'Do you really think it's inevitable that you'll get divorced?'

It was something I said to him one night before we were together, when we were meeting occasionally and talking intimately but I was evading the possibility of commitment. The reason I gave him was a disbelief in relationships, and I said what he was now quoting me as saying about divorce. We were in a fancy wine bar, the kind he liked and I found pretentious, drinking from giant, fragile glasses, sitting on bar stools facing each other. I said it and then I excused myself to go to the toilet and walked straight into a glass door. It hurt. It almost knocked me out. There was a party of people on the other side of the door, a wine-tasting, and several of the people from the party saw me and laughed, though one woman asked if I was okay. In fact, I was in agony, and for a few moments thought I would fall down. But I didn't. I made it to the toilet, the pain went away and I found my way back upstairs. Back on my bar stool, I told him what had happened and watched the tenderness flash over his face. He no longer had the heart to question my feelings on love or divorce.

Later, at the time when we were most together, when commitment was a solid thing between us, he brought it up again. We were talking about living together, how we might spend our lives.

He said, 'Remember when you said it was inevitable you would get divorced? You don't really think that, do you?'

I said, 'Yes, I remember – and then I walked straight into a glass door.'

He laughed until his eyes watered, and whatever fragile thing was beginning to emerge between us was shattered. Each of us could accept this physical metaphor for the meaning we needed. I didn't have to take responsibility for what I said and neither of us had to check if the other agreed.

For years I had been telling myself, when I was anxious in a relationship: 'He'll be a good dad', 'He'll be easy to live with' or 'It won't hurt too much once it's over.' I used to tell myself that was a good enough reason to stay with someone. Somehow it was easier to stay, if I thought I wouldn't be afraid to leave later. I told myself I was being pragmatic. I was lying, in fact, when I said I thought it was inevitable. That wasn't how I felt at all. I was just trying to modulate my fear.

We didn't mention the glass door this evening. Instead, he said something he hadn't said before, something that gave me a sense of the feelings he had for me, feelings I might have appreciated his honesty about when we were together. He said he felt sorry for me. He thought it was such a sad thing to say, that if I felt like that, then mightn't that contribute to the likelihood of it happening?

'Commitment is a choice,' he said.

That made me baulk – I asked him didn't he think there was a chance he might not be able to stay with someone either?

He said he felt sure he wouldn't get divorced. He was sure they would be able to work it out.

I gave him an example, an impromptu fantasy anecdote of a partner who didn't come home, said she would spend the weekend with him and their children but ended up staying late at work, spent holidays in virtual boardrooms, the depth of his loneliness.

He thought it was funny. It made him laugh. He said it wouldn't happen. 'We would work on it together,' he said. 'Besides, it will be different then. Commitment will be like the feeling of love you have for your brother or your parents. It will just be, there'll be no question of leaving.'

I thought, There is the impasse. That's where we're talking past each other.

I said, 'Perhaps what I mean is that I wouldn't be afraid to leave, I wouldn't stay just because of the commitment. I wouldn't stay just because I had stayed for so long.' I said commitment for me wasn't a contract, not a fixed thing between people but a living thing that could also die, that had to be nurtured and fed or it would starve.

I thought of you, how you had once told me that the

reason you left my mum was because she didn't go back to work after you had children – 'She broke the contract,' you said, never mind all the other contracts you broke – and felt more vehement, more certain of my feelings.

My ex-boyfriend smiled the smile he'd been smiling all night. 'But do you think you could stay with someone?' he said.

I looked at him and his smile and felt that I knew what he was thinking. He was goading me, I thought, and it hurt. I was caught between self-criticism and my earlier certainty, his smile ushering in my doubt.

I said, 'I know I could. If I wanted to.'

He kept smiling and smoking and sipped his whisky. I thought, What is this, a competition? I imagined him and his future partner, his determination to stay, his determination for it to be good, and possibly, his pride in staying when he didn't want to, in being the man he hoped he would be, in maintaining that honour, his magnanimity, though there was nothing left in society to say he had to. Possibly also his disappointment that it wasn't with me, that I was never going to be that person. I started to think about all the people who had come and gone in my life, not only in my adult relationships but when I was a child. Teachers, friends' parents, family friends and my mother's relationships had provided a revolving door of father figures, none of whom stayed in touch or showed any desire to maintain contact once it was no longer convenient. People came and went. The intensity of our feelings for them at the time had no bearing on how quickly or completely they left, or disappeared without notice. Leaving meant something completely different to me than it did to him. And I wasn't sure then which one of us I would prefer to be.

I remembered something else you said to me, when you were happy and drunk in the summer days of your illness: 'A good marriage is paradise on Earth.' What did you mean by that? What did it mean that you said that? You whose marriage I could not wish to emulate. I was about to share this with my ex-boyfriend, to see what he did with the fact of you having said it. But then he asked another question that cut straight into what I was thinking.

'Why do you think you do that?' he said. 'Change into someone else for a relationship?'

It was my turn to laugh.

I said, 'Why do you think? I spent my life trying to be someone else to make a man love me, I don't know how to do it any other way.'

Then I spoke quite freely about the thinking I'd been doing about you, about reading old emails between us and remembering what I was like, how I tried so hard to think the way you thought, like what you liked, that even my use of language felt constricted and immature and false. Reading those emails, I remembered something I had, since you died, tried to forget: that being with you was difficult, uncomfortable, that it robbed something major from my sense of self.

'I'd forgotten,' I told my ex-boyfriend, 'how inadequate he made me feel, because now that he's dead I always feel like I'm enough. The dad I remember, the dad I speak to, bring into conversation, he loves me absolutely and for exactly who I am. He's my champion. He accepts anything I say or feel or do. That wasn't my living dad at all. I spent my life trying to please him, trying to invent myself so he'd be interested in me. It's a reflex reaction now, I can't help it.'

He felt sorry for me again then, I could see it. Really sorry for me, and quite sad. He looked like he'd begun to pity me, which was helpful as it assuaged my guilt. At the same time I was aware of how angry he used to get when I imagined how he felt and believed my own stories, took my imagination as a guide to his reality. Perhaps he didn't feel sorry for me at all, perhaps it was a feeling that hadn't occurred to me that was in his eyes, in the absence of his smile. Perhaps it was my own self-pity I was witnessing. Perhaps I felt sorry for myself compared to him, for what I'd lacked, for these complicated feelings I had that he couldn't relate to. Either way, it seemed a sad, fruitless thing to him that I should have this problem of stepping behind a distorting lens any time I began a relationship.

Then he asked another question he had perhaps wanted to ask all along, but been afraid to when we were together. Or not so much afraid as too accepting of my version of the world for the question to occur to him.

He said, 'Why do you think you do that?'

'Do what?'

'Talk about him as though he's alive.'

That made me laugh with a real joy. It made me glad to think it – a gladness built partly out of my ex-boyfriend's incredulity and partly, if I'm honest, out of a kind of gloating, as though the question proved what I needed most to know: that you belonged to me, that no one else could come close, that even death couldn't destroy the bond between us. There I was, the greedy child, the abandoned daughter, the daddy's girl. I was drunk by then, felt in need of your protection. I remember thinking that my ex-boyfriend could go home and spend the weekend with his dad, while all I could do was go to the cemetery and chat to the grass growing on your grave. If he felt excluded, maybe part of me wished that he too could know what it felt like to be the one who wasn't completely loved.

I had stopped caring any more about the original reason for being here, I was glad only of the chance to think and speak.

I said, 'I guess because he does feel alive to me. His anecdotes turn up where my anecdotes should be. Even though he wasn't there when I was little, he was a huge presence. He formed so many of my ideas about the world, my values. His words come to me like my own memories. And he makes me laugh. And these stories are the stories of my life.'

He nodded.

I said, 'I think it's because now he's dead he's no longer a separate thing to me. If anyone is going to get to know me, they will get to know him as well.'

I was thinking about how it's true, and perhaps makes people uncomfortable, that I bring you up at every opportunity, that I reference you as casually and often as I reference *The Simpsons*, that in some ways my entire life is one giant arrow pointing back to you.

I said, 'That's part of it, you see.'

I was talking to myself, I realised, thinking aloud. The moment and the question and the distance between us had allowed me to think new things. I could admit at this moment that the feelings I had for you, the ways I spoke about you, were perhaps not healthy, were perhaps a defence, were perhaps not easy for a partner to stomach. I could see that my attachment to you, my love and protectiveness and the way I maintained a constant dialogue with you might be a way of avoiding intimacy with anyone else. As I was talking, I started to imagine that it was my ex-boyfriend talking about his mother this way, if she had died, and how I would feel about it. I understood then how it was a way of always keeping another person out. And then I felt afraid of myself, and wondered if he was right, if he was heading into an idyllic future with someone he would be able to stay with, while all I was doing was diving into your past, into memories of someone who'd never wanted me, who did almost anything he could to avoid spending time with me when he was alive.

We had come full circle back to our sharpness. It was getting hard to see how we would leave this evening without more, and increasingly fractious, arguments. We drank and smoked some more. We changed the subject. We talked about the roundabout below us, the cars and the white tops of buses moving like liquid past each other, how easy and impossible it seemed that each did not smash into the next.

Then it was late enough that we wanted to sleep and, partly out of habit and partly the recklessness of all this honesty, I said I would stay. I didn't feel guilty any more, though I felt far away from home and slightly sick from all the whisky. We brushed our teeth and went to bed.

It was hot, and impossible to sleep. My stomach hurt and my bladder stung. I couldn't lie flat on his sloping bed but kept rolling into him, though I didn't want to. And because of the sleeplessness, the waking and falling, I had several dreams. One of the dreams in particular was extremely vivid.

In the dream, I was with my ex-boyfriend. We had gone to Greece. I wanted to show him a place, a beautiful place that was special to me, a gorge of crystal waterfalls in the cement cliff between a disused casino and the beach. I explained it all to him, sincerely, the history of it, how I had gone here as a child, the magic we had infused it with, the wonder. We climbed up there. It was a challenge but finally we arrived. The glistening waters, the waterfall – all the things I couldn't believe were real, had been afraid were no more than memory – shone brighter than I could have imagined. I was awestruck. I asked what he thought. He said, 'Yeah, it's nice. I've seen a few places like this before.'

I woke up, the dream still clear in my head. I looked at him sleeping beside me. I thought that everything I had said to him was untrue, that without meaning to, I had lied again. It wasn't that I was pretending to be someone else for him, that in relationships by reflex I became what the other person wanted me to be. It was subtler than that, like a missing sense. What I kept getting wrong was thinking someone could see what I was showing them, when they couldn't. Believing we were looking in the same direction, when our eyes found different places altogether.

He'd said there were moments in our relationship when he felt like he was flying, we were just brilliant, that he felt sorry for other couples who weren't like us. I wondered if I could guess which times he was talking about, whether or not I would have chosen the same ones. Perhaps I glimpsed in those moments the better person he saw in me, but I didn't want or know how to be her for long. With you, too, I wanted so much to think that you knew me, that I pretended not to notice when I didn't recognise myself.

I lay there thinking this through until the orange halo

around his blackout blind told me it was morning. Then I brushed my teeth and got dressed and said goodbye.

Goodbye forever, that's what I thought. Thank you for being there.

How do you find a person who will really see you?

How can you tell if you are really seen?

How can you tell if you are really seeing them?

This is what my friend, lying on the Heath in the burning sunlight, talking about our dead parents, said to me – the thing he said that felt so important about losing his mother – the thing that made me want to change the subject, that sparked off all these questions in me. He said she made him feel at home in the world. She knew who he was. She really saw him. That's why he missed her so much.

I try to imagine, sometimes, who you saw there, what daughter you found when you looked at me. I wonder if the reason I never felt at home as her was the same reason it was so easy for you to leave. I don't know what will happen to her, that fraction of a child, if I walk away, stop waiting to meet you.

Perhaps you can look after her for me.

31st January 2019

F ive years and I've moved again but you're still in the
same place. I didn't take the train this time, I cycled
eight miles and locked my bike at the arched stone gate
where men in square black coats piped in red turn
frowns into the gentlest greeting. I know the way now.
Turn right past the heart-shaped headstone of the too-
young boy, over the fountain roundabout, the low trees
beyond the crematorium. I brought you three Ferrero
Rocher, ate two and left you one. Told you everything that
had happened since we last spoke, didn't try to hide my
good mood, restlessness, exhaustion.

You were lying there underneath me and I was wondering where you'd gone. You were lying there underneath
me and I was wondering how much of you was left.

Your hair?

Your eyes?

Your too-loose blue suit?

Your shoes?

Your bones? Bones can last at least part of forever.

It occurred to me that if I was given the chance I would
like to have one to keep, a rib or a femur or the socket
from your hip, the real one, not the metal one. One shard
of you. To hold its smooth whiteness in my palm, run it
over my lip, lay it on a shelf in my room.

'That's my dad's wrist,' I could say. Your right wrist. If I had a child I wouldn't begrudge her one of mine.

But in my new room I put away all signs of you. I arrive and begin to unpack – nineteen banana boxes gratefully acquired from Morrisons on Holloway Road and packed with books, clothes, records, the detritus of my life. But taking out the clay letters spelling 'Holy Spirit' that I made for you, halfway through unwrapping them from newspaper, I stop.

I don't know where to put them. I don't know if there's room. I don't know if I want to look at them. I don't know if I want them.

I don't want them. They're yours.

They're yours.

For four years they posed as mine. I have stared at them on the top of my bookcase and I have stared at your deadness on the top of my bookcase and you have been dead there, on the top of my bookcase, like I needed proof of the end of your life.

I did need proof. It was a hard fact to hold on to.

But this was a new room, new November, new version of my life. I realised I didn't have to put them up again. So I didn't. I wrapped them back in newspaper and put them back in the box. Along with:

Your photograph.

Your armadillo watercolour painting.

Your stick you brought back from Greece.

Your old shirts.

Your letters.

Your notebooks.

Your biro.

Your wooden fork.

Why did I have all these things, so many of them indistinguishable from rubbish? Had I been living inside a shrine to you for years?

I thought about someone I had brought home to my old room, how he had been troubled by the poem of yours that hung over my bed, how his eyes flickered up to it often and how he seemed to flinch as though he'd caught me flirting with a stranger every time I mentioned your name.

But your name wasn't 'my dad', was it?

Not Daddy either.

Sebastian?

My mother used to call you Seb.

As a child, you were known as Bashie. That's what your mother calls you in her diaries, in her letters, your sister too. Bashie. Because you were always climbing on things and leaping off, falling down, cracking your head, indifferent.

Sebastian Barker, he's a poet. Or just SSB, carved into the thin plywood box of pens and scissors and scalpels on your desk.

I want to sit beside you at that desk again. I want to play with the sticky sheet of fake leather that rolls up at the edges. I want to smell the pencil sharpenings and ink and paper, glue from the spines of books, your shirts, your hair, your shoulder when you hugged me to you.

I want the sunlight coming in through the window, the foxes prowling in the garden below, the wood pigeons calling, the light coming in, my brother and I dangling from our fingertips along the metal crossbeam in the ceiling more than twenty years ago.

These are the things I can't put in a box. These are the things I can't take out of a box. These are the things I can't hang over my bed for any stranger to contemplate or confuse.

I want you and I don't want you. I want you outside of me. I want you as something far away that I can visit when I choose to, not this personal haunting we've kept up.

Here I was in a new room where there was no man, no other, for the first time in years. Just me and my belongings and yours. And all yours I put back in their box.

Five years is half a decade. The length of time children are permitted to play and grow before the constraints of school.

Long enough for your body to decay. Is it your body I miss the most?

No.

And it's not the way you looked at me, either, not the way a room felt with the two of us in it.

334

Not the way you laughed so seriously and made small things extraordinary.

Not the words you used, your fables and stories. Not the aphorisms you threw around as your guiding principles for life. Not your fountain-pen letters or your oil paintings or your plans.

Not the apples you kept in your car, the broken things you fixed that turned out better.

Not your joy in the things most people would throw away.

Not your toughness, your coolness, your resilience, your predictability.

Not your hand holding a glass of green wine in the evening sunlight, your croaking voice singing Townes van Zandt.

Not your handmade gifts, or your letters, or the endless stream of knowledge you tried to give me.

It's not any of the things I used to miss the most. All that was a decoy, an attachment to memory, to the past. These things are no further away than any other fragments of the past, as my mother or brother that many years ago. As so many things it is necessary to let go. No. What I miss most is having you here in the future with me, not as you were then, but as you would have been: the continuation of you, the one we'll never know.

I don't know what you would make of who I am now. In fact, this knowledge is impossible since who I am is made out of your death. So what I miss the most is those

335

two people – you, alive, here, with more life ahead of you, and that other version of me, the one who still loves and hates you, still moves in and out of your life, still doesn't know the answer is never going to arrive.

Instead I have you inked on my body: your coelacanth tattooed on my ribs. Cyril, you christened him, pronounced 'Seye-ril' because you always had to say words your own way. Pressed off the paper into my skin by a slow-moving woman with weightless hands who listened to the story until my throat closed with pain, then folded my words into her own. I watched the needle's shadow dance with hers over the carpet, counting my breath, for two hours or more. The sensation was so intense I felt I could see the needle scraping at bone, my blood mixing into the drawing, that it was more than ink she was knitting into my skin.

There he swims still, moving with my breath, swimming under my clothes while I walk and lie and stretch and sleep. And the fact that you hated tattoos is just another way I'm teasing you, spiting you still, making you scowl-smile. Because I won't forget all the spikiness between us, no matter how easy it was, in the end, for love to absorb all that. Cyril swims and I watch you breathing in your deathless fish, thought extinct for eighty million years but all the time alive, indifferent, at the bottom of the ocean.

You were lying there underneath me and I was wondering where you'd gone, if the grass was still green because of you or if there was more than sunlight in every yellow smudge of paint.

I don't miss you

W hat happened?
       You lived, you died, we met each other.

You built a house and loved several women including my mother and had four children and spoke to us. And sometimes hurt us. And sometimes ignored us. And sometimes made the world a completely different place.

You died twice, I think.

I could argue for more. Perhaps my mother would. But I make it twice.

My dad died twice.

The first time, on 31st January 2014, I did not believe and scoffed at. Your body was there, yes, too cold and too still, and I touched your hand, pushed a twig from one of the olive trees in our garden in Greece between your stiff fingers, listened to the undertaker on the phone through the thin walls, wondered about grief laid out like this, what anybody would or could do in that room.

They buried you.

I remember the men in their black coats hauling on the ropes to lower you down. I had not imagined the logistics of it that modern technology cannot alter. The mud. The hole. The rain. The cold. 19th February 2014. And I almost laughed and stood there shaking my head inside, thinking, These people are crazy, they know nothing.

I did not believe you had died then.

I don't believe you died then. Not for me. You stayed with me.

You were at my shoulder all that summer. I spoke to you in every empty room I found myself in, and in some rooms that weren't empty. I cycled across London in the burning heat calling your name to the sky, the pavement, laughing at myself and my euphoria. I felt your hand on my head. I felt you smiling above me. I felt you watching and accepting everything I did. I had never felt that kind of love from you before, and I basked in it, could not understand all that I'd heard about death.

And then I would miss you. Gone, again. The shock of it. Crying on my bedroom floor. The smell of carpet. The finality of it.

Gone, gone, gone.

I went to visit your grave and walked around in an eye-stinging daze, you following behind pointing out the paths and trees and shrubs criss-crossing your new residence, and did and did not believe it.

But that was years ago. The second time you died was closer than that. October 2017. I felt you slipping away. I felt that it was all right. I understood that you had to leave then. And if it was painful at first, if the world felt duller and emptier, it was a relief too, not to carry you everywhere I went.

Now your absence is like a bruise I have to keep pressing to make sure the pain is still there.

I don't speak to you any more. Not in the same way. If I speak to you now I am speaking to myself. It is no longer true if I say: my dad is not dead. It's not that I've lost the conviction, but that I've lost the last living part of you. I wonder about it.

I don't miss you.

I do.

For weeks and months I feel nothing. Your anniversary passes and I don't feel sad at all. I forget your birthday. I see a photo of you and it is only that – one captured moment. And then something happens that I want to tell you about, or I tell a story about you I had forgotten, and all at once your goneness is brutal again.

I don't like missing you, that's the truth of it. It's uncomfortable. It makes me feel hollow and ungrounded, distant from the living people I care about. So it's not as though I don't miss you, the rest of the time, but that I had to learn how to let go of that feeling, to step away from the bereft daughter and look out of another window in myself. After however many years treading around in here, it's easy enough to find the space.

I don't miss you when I'm brushing my teeth. I don't miss you when I'm having breakfast, except when I eat toast, which is rarely. I don't miss you when I'm at work – when I'm with children, I miss nothing and no one. I don't miss you when I'm lying on the scratchy yellow grass in the park eating a fridge-cold apple watching the sun turn the evening pink. I don't miss you when I'm listening to Arcade Fire or Michael Kiwanuka or anyone else you've never heard of. I don't miss you when I'm in a room with my closest friends, someone's particular laugh, someone else's outrage, that special knowledge of each other. I don't miss you when I'm putting my shoes on, as long as the laces are already tied. If I have to tie the laces and have a second to think, I think of the mechanical ingenuity of fingers tying laces and the small-scale awe it fills me with leads me straight back to you. Then I miss you, but mostly I'm lazy and leave my laces tied. I don't miss you when I'm running. I don't miss you when I'm doing the washing-up, even if I remember what you said about it, I just want to get it done before my skin starts to itch. I don't miss you when I'm watching TV, except on those lovely dull nights when I'm watching alone, looking for something unremarkable that nobody would think to talk about and I remember that funny thing about you, that you liked B movies better than any others and watched daytime TV as much as you could when you weren't lost in a poetry firestorm. I don't miss you when I happen to be waiting at your local over-ground station and a freight train passes through, blasting everything from me except its rush of shapes and noise. I don't miss you when I'm not thinking about you, which nowadays, admittedly, is quite often. I didn't think that would happen but it did.

I don't miss you when I'm walking through Abney Park with someone I can't get enough of talking to, don't even notice your memory wafting through the graves to hide in the ivy-covered trees, don't listen to the voice that wants to say out loud the line from your poem about here, don't care that you first brought me here. I don't miss you when we walk past the town hall where your wake was, or the pub we drank too much in after. I don't miss you when we go in there for a drink and I tell him and he seems shocked and sad and asks if I mind us being there. I tell him no, it's fine, it was ages ago. I think then I don't miss you at all. But then that 'ages ago' hovers in my head for days. You are ages ago. Years and years. It's hard to believe sometimes that you were ever alive at all. You aren't alive to the person I'm talking to. To him, you've been dead forever. And I miss you then, angry at how wrong it is, that the small fact of your goneness should wipe out every other aspect of you.

I miss you when the same person asks me about your funeral. We're talking about funerals, and I mention yours. I start to talk and then it begins, the familiar shake inside. It's as though my current state of mind, the one I've been carrying long enough to imagine I've always felt this way, is only a rented room in a house that's beginning to sink into the ground. I'm still talking about your funeral but the words I'm saying have become false, everything I thought has become untrue. I miss you just as much as I ever did. There's nothing else.

I miss you all the way through the gig we're at – the feeling hijacks the meaning of each song. I miss you all the way to the bottom of my third glass of wine that I'm only drinking because it reminds me of you. I miss you every time I drink red wine. I miss you every time I end up in Soho. I miss you every time I see your sister. I miss you every time I go to Greece. I miss you every time I see a fox, or a wood pigeon, or a friendly dog with no apparent owner. I miss you every time I use a hammer. I miss you every time I say the word 'anathema'. I miss you every time I'm walking somewhere and take out my phone to ring someone and realise again, as though it might not have been true, that the number I have saved with your photo is out of service, I can't even leave you a voicemail if I wanted to. I miss you every time I think that I don't miss you, and after that I miss you more and more. A boulder rolls in, dismantling everything. I miss you, but then my mind glazes over and I try again to remember what better things I have to do. It's as though after so many years all that's happened is that I've learned to trust I will miss you again. I don't have to guard the feeling so closely, because no matter how long I lose it, it'll always find its way back.

I don't miss you when I'm getting dressed. I don't miss you when I'm in the supermarket. I don't miss you when I'm on my bike, even though that was the place I used to talk to you the most after you died. I don't miss you when I'm listening to the radio, or watching the news, or reading, though every now and then it occurs to me that you might have thought this or that about something, and then I miss you, proportionately to how much I wish I'd heard you say it. Other times, all that occurs to me is the fact that you don't know about this. The present, and every day since you've died, is a total mystery to you. You'll never know how far I went in search of you.

You'll never know that last summer I went to the South of France to find the cave paintings you talked about for so long. You won't know that I took the train to Toulouse, stayed in a nearby town, took a bus and walked six kilometres up a dirt track to the crack in the mountain of Pech Merle. You won't know how scared I was, alone in the unfamiliar mountains, trying to ensure no strangers saw which way I went. I don't know how you got there, if you trod the same track, wondered at its narrowness or the invisible threads that hung there. You don't know the panic I felt to discover myself covered in what I thought were maggots, the sudden idea that in my trek to your death I was being eaten alive. You might have laughed, pointed out they were only caterpillars – fat and soft and green. You won't know that they rode my arms and legs all the way to the site, with its ticket office and gift shop, where I found a bench and shared my lunch with the wasps. You won't know how much I missed you, hearing your voice, watching for your shadow, wondering what you did there. You won't know how grateful I was when my ticket was called and I had to concentrate on the narrow staircase, on not tripping and falling into the rock.

I should have known how much I'd miss you there. The air was dank, cold and shivery. The light flickered. To see the horses that you'd spoken about, the red hand-prints, the buffalo, the black blown shapes of the paintings – time is a rolling pin pushed across your mind. I looked and thought and felt inadequate to looking, felt my thoughts dissolve to nothing. I wondered why I'd come so far just to see what you'd seen, when there was no journey I could make that would turn my eyes into yours.

But then something particular happened.

As we were guided through, stopping at various spots to listen to the guide's explanations, a man kept turning up beside me. He might have been seventy-five, eighty years old. We were a large crowd, twenty-five people, old couples, families with young children, families with teen-agers, and me – the only solo visitor, perhaps, unless this man was alone also. I couldn't tell who he was with, and that was partly what made him stand out. We were led through the passages, given explanations of the paintings, wandering through the stalagmites and stalactites. He kept appearing beside me. We didn't acknowledge each other. We were in no order, though I didn't find myself so often beside anybody else. I would smell his smell, hear his breath, feel the vibrations of it, and know he was there. His breathing was heavy and, more than the caves themselves, he smelled of death: an underground smell of decay, mushrooms, inanimate bodies, recycled air. His mouth hung open, his hands clasped behind his back in a way that looked uncomfortable to me but seemed natural to him – perhaps this is what must be done with hands painful and thick with arthritis. My younger hands clutched my bag, my pockets, my shorts. He leaned in close beside me every time we stopped to see a painting. So while I saw every prehistoric painting, I also took in close-ups of his face. His jowls and dry lips. His nose. The long hairs of his eyebrows. His glassy eyes that did not blink. His gaze fixed over my shoulder. We watched together. None of the other people watched as long as us, perhaps that was why we ended up repeatedly together. The others walked on. He said nothing. We were the silent ones, while the parents and children and couples made caveman jokes, called out for echoes.

The guide took us to a section of the cave known for incredible acoustics and suggested someone sing, and immediately every teenager turned to their mother and said, 'Don't, it's so embarrassing.' There was laughter. But not from the man or me. He was tall and thin and hunched forward, watching the damp walls, the 25,000-year-old handprints in iron ore. I loved him being there, and because he kept appearing where I stood, I wondered if he loved me being there also.

I wondered if he had been waiting inside the cave for me.

I wondered if anyone else could see him.

I wondered if he was you.

He might have been – you who walked there over a decade before, and were not so old then, but would almost have been as old as him now, as though you had been waiting down here all that time. I tried to imagine you his age, and could easily do so. You would have been like him. And what would have become of the two of us, talking or walking together a hundred feet under-ground in the damp, prehistoric air, silent in the dull yellow light? Would it have been like it was with that old man, you following me, and not the other way around? I wonder if those two doppelgängers are down there still. Outside in the daylight, I didn't see him again. And I didn't miss you, either. I didn't miss you all the way back down the mountain. I was only glad to be outside, alive in the sunlight with a map and no one, not even a dead man, to talk to. I didn't miss you all the rest of that trip.

I used to live in a shrine to you. But in this new room all I have are your books, lined up with so many others, easy to miss. The room I mourned you in belongs to someone else. I didn't want to leave it but I'm glad I can't go back. Too much had happened in that room. I moved there two weeks before you died. I made you spanakopitas in that kitchen. The shelves you made me were fitted to the wall. In that room I hallucinated you, dreamed you, wrote all these words about you. I stared out of that window thinking about you, smoking and watching the pigeons, tracing the chaos of Seven Sisters Road, the roof of the casino, the Morrisons car park, the Nag's Head market, all those years since you had been alive. I kept staring until I could not tell you apart from the concrete or the fire escapes, could not distinguish grief from what the city lights did to the sky.

You know now that I love you. I know now that you love me. I don't need your journals, your paintings, your poems. I don't need to talk about you every day. I don't need to drag you like a cover over myself to shelter from everyone else I meet. I don't need you, either, do I? Like you said, I'm old enough.

I used to think that I would give anything, take anything, accept all the hurtful things you did, forgive all the pain you caused, if I could see you one more time. I used to think that anything would be worth it. I would have traded my home, my job, working limbs, boyfriends, for one more conversation with you. I don't think that any more. I don't want it. I want what happened after. I want the consequences of all the pain and trying you wrought in me, not the pain and trying all over again. To want you back now is to want to return to the past, and no matter how much I love you, how huge and complicated the scope of that love, the honest thing to say is that I needed to let you die, and to let all those incommensurate parts drift apart.

Trying to be a daughter to you was like holding together the shards of a broken window. But it's not so painful any more. So I want you to stay now, as you are. Because I love all of you, the bad parts and the good parts, the parts I conjure and the parts I don't like to remember, I need you to stay where this is possible. I need you to stay where I can find the parts of you in different places, pull them up from the deep and rub the dirt of time off them one at a time. Another day with you would mean bringing it all together, and that is exactly what will break it apart.

So I'll leave you there, and you can wait for me in our house you built, with the bleached coke can and driftwood, the shards of cup and all your cassette tapes. I'll open the door to let the mountain in, sit on the door-step planning with my brother how to fix the cracked beams, keep the rain out, make it a place we want to be. I wonder if you'll recognise us, or the home we make there, once we finish what you started.

Acknowledgements

The writing of this book began more times than I can remember, but it would never have made it beyond the scraps of notes and possibilities without the faith and encouragement of Cathy Rentzenbrink. Thank you for giving me the tools to make the space for it to happen. Thank you also to everyone at Spread the Word, in particular Bobby Nayyar, for introducing me to Cathy and for all your support and enthusiasm following the Life Writing prize. Special thanks to Kwaku Osei-Afrifa for seeing something in 'Paradoxical' and for an invaluable conversation.

Thank you to my editor, Mary-Anne Harrington, for seeing what I was doing and what it could be, and for asking the right questions to take it there. Thank you also for your kindness and wisdom regarding working around the wild and unpredictable life of a small baby. Thanks to everyone at Tinder Press for their sensitive work on each aspect of the book.

I'm especially grateful to my agent Milly Reilly for

holding my hand through this process and fielding all my anxieties along the way. A wave of appreciation to everyone at JULA for your enthusiasm and warmth and for fostering a sense of community at an isolating time.

Scott Manley Hadley, Harry Gallon, Jonathan McAloon and Max Sydney Smith all read early versions of this book or parts of it. I'm indebted to all of you for your time, wit, editorial and emotional insight and probably a number of small beers. Thank you to Emily Palmer and Danielle Manning for reading the manuscript when I was afraid of looking at it and understanding what it meant. Thank you Angela Easby for another helpful conversation. A big thank you also to Sean Preston for providing a baseline of encouragement for almost a decade.

A cacophony of thank yous and more to Emily Palmer, Danielle Manning, Christina Photiou, Alice Mckeever, Gabriella Boyd, Hannah Tuson, Julia Martin, Anya Broido, Camilla MacSwiney, Lia Ikkos, Gabriella McGrogan and Julie Tanner for being around, for talking to me, for laughing and all the other serious friend stuff, and to Rebecca Lanham for all of that plus living with me and our silent six o'clock in the mornings. Thank you to everyone who's listened to me talk about my dad over the years and everyone who shared with me their own stories.

When I started writing most of the pieces that are in this book I never imagined it would be published, and that gave me a certain recklessness about what I was willing or able to put into words. But now it's here, an object in the world, with realities inside it that share in more lives than my own. So I'm forever indebted and thankful to my family and to everybody else mentioned in these pages. I tried as far as possible to write through a lens that focused solely on my own relationship with my dad and left everyone else as outlines, but to my mum I owe incalculable gratitude for her generosity and empathy. To my brother, too – thank you.

Finally Chris, you're here, thank you! And to Seaghdh, for being part of things.